I0454308

List of Contents

Introduction

In a world brimming with business jargon and marketing strategies, it's easy to get lost amidst the noise of catchphrases and bold claims. Companies, all claiming to be "customer-centric," vie for your attention and your loyalty. But what does it truly mean to be customer-centric? Is it just another catchy phrase, or does it hold the key to building lasting success in the competitive landscape of modern business?

As you open the pages of this book you're about to find the secret that will unveil the mysteries of customer loyalty and reveal the transformative potential that lies within your customer base. This book isn't about vague promises or empty slogans; it's about practical strategies, tangible steps, and real-world success stories that have withstood the test of time.

In a landscape where trends ebb and flow, where the business world can feel like a chaotic storm of change, one constant remains: the power of the customer. It's an age-old truth that transcends technology, economic shifts, and marketing gimmicks. Customers are the lifeblood of any business, the vital force that sustains the entire operation. But, dear reader, we're not here to discuss just any customers. We're here to uncover the secret of loyal customers – those who not only return to your business but become your brand's most ardent advocates.

Loyal customers are your unsung sales force, quietly influencing others through the powerful medium of word-of-mouth marketing. They're not merely patrons; they're brand champions. They're not just consumers; they're creators of trust. And in these pages, you'll learn how to transform everyday customers into these extraordinary, loyal ambassadors for your business.

Now, you might be thinking, "Why should I care about this concept of 'loyalty'? I'm here to boost sales, increase revenue, and grow my business." Well, you're absolutely right. That's precisely what we're going to achieve together. The magic of loyalty is that it doesn't merely increase your bottom line; it amplifies it. Loyal customers spend more, stay longer, and tell the world about your business – all of which translates into a healthier, more prosperous venture.

This book isn't here to dazzle you with the latest trends or entangle you in convoluted theories. It's here to provide you with practical, straightforward, and actionable insights on how to build, attract, and retain loyal customers. It's about getting down to the nitty-gritty of what works in the real world, devoid of corporate jargon or empty rhetoric.

In the pages ahead, we'll delve deep into the essence of customer loyalty. You'll learn that it's not merely a result of rewards programs or discounts, but the outcome of genuine connections forged through understanding and empathy. You'll discover how to craft an irresistible customer experience that leaves an indelible mark on your customers' hearts and minds. We'll explore the power of customer feedback, a tool often overlooked, but one that can drive continuous improvement and foster a sense of customer involvement.

But we won't stop there. This book isn't just about retaining customers; it's about converting them into your most potent marketing force. You'll unravel the secrets of creating brand advocates, those individuals who shout your praises from the rooftops. And it doesn't stop at testimonials; we'll investigate the powerful influence of social proof and reviews in building trust and credibility.

We'll also explore the concept of going beyond customer expectations. It's about creating experiences so remarkable that customers are not only delighted but left with no option but to return and bring others along for the experience. You'll uncover the steps to instill a customer-centric culture in your organization, where every employee is a champion of customer satisfaction and positive interactions.

But we're not done yet. We will continues as we delve into the art of converting these loyal customers into your sales force. You'll understand that loyalty is not just an outcome; it's the beginning of an entirely new chapter. By the time we're through, you'll be well-versed in the strategies, techniques, and tactics to turn your customers into your most effective sales advocates.

You see, there's a profound shift happening in the world of business. It's a shift from traditional advertising and marketing to the realm of authenticity and advocacy. It's a movement that doesn't rely on pushy ads or interruptive tactics; it's powered by the trust and respect of loyal customers who willingly promote your brand. They're the voices that matter most in today's marketplace.

As you turn the pages of this book, imagine that I'm there with you, sharing stories, insights, and practical advice like a trusted friend and mentor. This isn't just another business book; it's a guide that will empower you to take your business to the next level.

Let's unlocking the secrets to not just attracting and retaining loyal customers, but converting them into your most potent sales force. Welcome to the path of lasting success and unshakable brand loyalty. Let's get started.

Chapter 1: The Customer-Centric Mindset

1.1 The Power of Customer-Centricity

In the fiercely competitive landscape of the modern business world, one thing stands out as a critical differentiator between thriving enterprises and those merely struggling to survive: customer-centricity. This shift in focus is not just a trend; it's a strategic imperative that has the potential to reshape the very essence of your business and its future. Let's dive deep into why customer-centricity matters and how it has become the linchpin of success in today's marketplace.

Why Customer-Centricity Matters

At its core, a customer-centric approach is about making your customers the focal point of every decision you make. It's a mindset that reframes how you view your business operations. Instead of obsessing over products, services, or sales figures, you prioritize understanding, meeting, and exceeding the needs of your customers.

Why does this matter so much? Well, the answer is simple: without customers, your business is just a hollow shell. No matter how groundbreaking your products or innovative your services, they're all irrelevant if you don't have a customer base to appreciate and utilize them.

Customer-centricity takes this understanding a step further. It's not just about having customers; it's about keeping them, nurturing their loyalty, and turning them into your most ardent advocates. And that's where the magic happens. When you commit to putting your customers first, not only do you create loyal patrons, but you also establish a sustainable foundation for growth.

Consider this: in an era where choices are abundant, customers no longer gravitate toward companies that focus solely on their bottom line. They seek something more profound - a brand that resonates with their values and delivers an experience that goes beyond the transaction. This is why customer-centricity matters. It's the compass that guides your business toward long-term, sustainable success.

Furthermore, customer-centricity is the key to unlocking invaluable insights into your audience. By making a conscious effort to understand their needs, preferences, and pain points, you gain a competitive edge. You're not just selling; you're creating solutions. And these solutions aren't hypothetical; they're rooted in real customer feedback and experiences.

In today's data-driven world, customers expect to be heard. They want to feel like their voices matter. It's no longer enough to offer a product or service; you must offer an ear to listen and adapt based on what you hear. By actively incorporating customer feedback, you demonstrate your commitment to continuous improvement, and in doing so, you strengthen the foundation of trust.

The Shift from Product to Customer Focus

Traditionally, businesses were product-centric. The focus was on creating the best possible product and pushing it into the market. Companies would invest heavily in research and development to bring innovative products to the forefront, and the assumption was that if the product was excellent, customers would come.

However, the dynamics have changed drastically. With increased competition and easier access to information, customers have grown more discerning. It's no longer sufficient to have a great product; it's about whether that product aligns with what the customer wants and values. The customer is no longer willing to be a passive recipient of whatever a business offers.

This shift from product to customer focus is a seismic change. It places the customer at the center of your business universe. Everything you do, from product development to marketing, revolves around their needs and desires.

By understanding your customers at a deep level, you can tailor your products or services to precisely meet their requirements. It's about offering them not just what they want but what they didn't know they wanted. It's the art of pre-empting their needs and providing solutions before they even realize they have a problem. This proactive approach is the hallmark of a customer-centric business.

This shift is not just about giving customers what they want. It's also about what they need. It's about connecting with them on an emotional level, understanding their motivations, and resonating with their values. The product is no longer the hero of the story; the customer is.

The Benefits of a Customer-Centric Approach

Now, you might be wondering what's in it for your business when you embrace a customer-centric approach. The benefits are substantial, and they ripple through every aspect of your operations.

First and foremost, customer-centricity breeds loyalty. When customers feel seen and heard, they develop a deep-rooted connection with your brand. They're not merely satisfied; they're emotionally invested. These loyal customers become your brand advocates, spreading positive word-of-mouth and influencing others. They are, in essence, your unpaid sales force.

But the advantages don't stop there. A customer-centric approach also leads to increased customer retention. In a competitive market, retaining existing customers is often more cost-effective than acquiring new ones. Satisfied and loyal customers are more likely to stick around, reducing churn and saving you resources that can be redirected towards growth.

Customer-centricity fosters innovation. By actively listening to your customers, you gain insights that can shape your product development and marketing strategies. You create products that address real needs, not perceived ones. This, in turn, leads to more satisfied customers and a growing market share.

Additionally, a customer-centric approach enhances your brand's reputation. Businesses known for their customer-centric mindset are viewed as trustworthy and transparent. This enhances your brand's credibility, making it more appealing to both customers and potential partners.

By placing your customers at the center of every decision, shifting from a product to a customer focus, and reaping the benefits of loyalty, retention, and innovation, you can transform your business into a powerful, customer-driven force in the marketplace. It's a transformation that holds the potential to redefine your future and elevate your brand to new heights.

1.2 Understanding Your Audience

In the realm of business, understanding your audience is akin to holding a compass as you navigate a dense forest – it's your guide to making informed decisions and reaching your destination successfully. In this section, we delve into the intricate art of comprehending your audience, a crucial facet of the customer-centric mindset that serves as the foundation for attracting and retaining loyal customers.

Creating Customer Personas

Imagine a painter preparing to create a masterpiece. They don't start with a blank canvas and randomly splash paint around; they begin with a vision. The same principle applies when you seek to understand your audience. You start with a vision of your ideal customer – a persona that represents the characteristics, desires, and needs of a segment of your target market.

Creating customer personas involves delving deep into the demographics, psychographics, and behaviors of your customers. It's not just about knowing their age, gender, and location; it's about uncovering what keeps them up at night, what motivates their decisions, and what problems they yearn to solve. A well-crafted persona is a vivid, detailed representation of your customer – not an abstract concept, but a real person with real aspirations.

Why is this important? Because it empowers you to tailor your offerings to meet their specific needs. Think of it as a bespoke suit tailored to fit perfectly – a personalized experience for your customers. It's about showing that you know them, that you've walked in their shoes, and that you're here to make their lives better.

Consider Sarah, a fictional persona for a tech-savvy millennial. She's in her late twenties, lives in a bustling city, and values convenience, eco-friendliness, and staying connected. Armed with this information, a business can create products and services that cater to Sarah's preferences. They might offer an app for quick and eco-friendly transportation, a loyalty program that rewards her tech-savvy choices, and customer service that understands her need for immediacy.

Segmenting Your Target Market

Imagine a vast, bustling marketplace. Within it, you'll find diverse groups of people, each with distinct preferences and needs. In business, your market is no different. It's a mosaic of unique segments, and to truly understand your audience, you must be adept at segmenting your target market.

Segmentation is like creating sections in that bustling marketplace, organizing customers into groups based on shared characteristics. These characteristics can be demographic, geographic, psychographic, or behavioral. It's the process of acknowledging that one size doesn't fit all, and recognizing the nuances of each customer group.

Why is segmentation crucial? It allows you to allocate your resources wisely. Instead of attempting a one-size-fits-all approach, you can tailor your marketing and product strategies to address the specific needs and desires of each segment. It's like a chef preparing different dishes for various tastes, ensuring that everyone leaves the restaurant satisfied.

Let's take a look at an example. Consider a company that sells outdoor adventure gear. They've identified two distinct segments in their target market: the thrill-seekers and the nature enthusiasts. Thrill-seekers crave adrenaline-pumping experiences and cutting-edge equipment, while nature enthusiasts prefer eco-friendly, sustainable products and serene, low-impact adventures.

By segmenting their market, this company can create two tailored marketing campaigns. The thrill-seekers receive enticing offers for extreme adventures and high-performance gear, while the nature enthusiasts are drawn in with messages of sustainability and tranquil, nature-centric experiences. This level of personalization speaks directly to each segment's unique desires, creating a deeper connection.

Tailoring Products and Services to Customer Needs
Imagine you're attending a restaurant renowned for its personalized service. The waitstaff remembers your favorite dish, adjusts the level of spice just how you like it, and suggests new menu items that align with your tastes. This is what it means to tailor products and services to customer needs – providing a seamless, customized experience that leaves your customers feeling valued and understood.

To excel at this, you must first grasp what your customers truly need and desire. This doesn't come from assumptions or guesswork but from the careful analysis of data, feedback, and a willingness to actively listen to your customers. It means understanding the problems they face and finding solutions that fit like a glove.

Why is this level of tailoring important? It's about creating a product or service that aligns perfectly with what your customers are seeking, even if they don't explicitly express it. It's about making their lives easier, more enjoyable, or more efficient. When customers find what they're looking for in your offerings, they'll become loyal supporters, returning again and again.

Let's consider the example of a digital streaming service. By analyzing user data and feedback, they discover that a significant portion of their audience loves vintage black-and-white movies. In response, they create a "Classics Collection" with carefully curated old films and a user-friendly interface. The result? These customers feel like the service was designed just for them, and their loyalty deepens.

When you understand your customers on this level, you're poised to create experiences that resonate deeply, forging bonds that stand the test of time.

1.3 Building Empathy and Relationships

In today's business landscape, where the competitive tides are constantly shifting, one thing remains constant: the paramount importance of the customer. It's no secret that customers are the lifeblood of any business, the driving force behind its growth and success. In the pages that follow, we delve into the heart of what it means to be truly customer-centric, starting with the critical role of empathy and building enduring relationships with those who sustain your enterprise.

The Role of Empathy in Customer-Centricity

Empathy, a simple yet profoundly powerful concept, lies at the core of customer-centricity. It's the art of understanding the world through your customer's eyes, stepping into their shoes, and comprehending their needs, concerns, and desires. It's the ability to listen, not just with your ears, but with your heart. And it's more than a buzzword; it's a skill that can transform the way you do business.

Think about the last time you were genuinely listened to, your concerns validated, and your needs addressed. How did it make you feel? Valued, respected, and appreciated, I'd bet. Empathy in business is akin to offering someone a seat at the table of respect and understanding. It creates a space where customers aren't just a number on a balance sheet; they are real people with real problems and aspirations.

Empathy isn't about empty phrases or scripted responses. It's about sincerity and a commitment to solving your customer's problems, even if it means going above and beyond. When your customers realize that you genuinely care about their well-being, you're not just securing their loyalty; you're earning their trust. And trust, my friend, is the cornerstone of any lasting relationship.

But empathy isn't a one-time act. It should permeate every aspect of your business, from product development to customer service. It's not about fixing what's broken; it's about anticipating what could break and addressing it proactively. It's about knowing your customers so well that you can predict their needs before they even recognize them themselves. And when you consistently meet their needs, you're more than a business; you're a trusted partner.

Nurturing Long-Term Customer Relationships

If empathy is the foundation of customer-centricity, then nurturing long-term customer relationships is the sturdy framework upon which that foundation is built. In a world where competition is fierce and choices abound, customers don't stick around for average service or mediocre products. They stay loyal when they feel a connection, when they feel seen and valued, and when they believe that their relationship with you is more than a transaction.

To nurture long-term customer relationships, you must be willing to invest in them. It's not a one-way street; it's a partnership. It means making the effort to understand your customer's preferences, needs, and behaviors. It means remembering their names, their previous purchases, and their birthdays. It means treating them like friends, not just customers.

Imagine you have a friend who remembers your favorite coffee order and surprises you with it when you meet. It's a small gesture, but it leaves a big impact. In the world of business, these gestures can be personalized recommendations, exclusive offers, or early access to new products. These are the touches that make customers feel that you value their business and appreciate their loyalty.

Additionally, consistency is key to nurturing long-term relationships. Trust is built on predictability. If your customers experience a seamless, satisfying interaction every time they engage with your business, they will learn to rely on you. This consistency isn't just about the quality of your products or services; it's about the consistency of your values, your commitment to customer satisfaction, and your dedication to making their lives better.

The Human Connection in Business

In our increasingly digital world, it's easy to forget the power of the human touch. But the truth is, even in the age of automation and artificial intelligence, the human connection remains invaluable. There's a reason why people prefer to speak to a real person when they have a problem; it's the human connection, the assurance that someone understands and cares.

In the realm of customer-centricity, the human connection is what sets you apart from the faceless, soulless corporations. It's about creating an environment where your customers feel like they're communicating with a friend, not a chatbot or an automated response. It's about understanding that behind every email, every call, and every transaction is a person with their own set of challenges and aspirations.

The human connection is about being available when your customers need you. It's about being empathetic and responsive. It's about actively seeking feedback, listening to their concerns, and taking swift action to address their issues. It's about making them feel heard and appreciated.

A powerful human connection can turn a mere customer into an advocate, someone who not only continues to do business with you but also actively promotes your brand to others. And in the business world, this is gold.

The customer-centric mindset begins with empathy, a fundamental understanding that the customer is at the core of your business's success. Nurturing long-term relationships with your customers takes that empathy and turns it into action. It transforms mere transactions into meaningful interactions, ensuring that your customers don't just come back to your business; they become its most passionate advocates. And through it all, the human connection remains the glue that binds it together, reminding us that in the realm of business, the most enduring and valuable relationships are the ones built on trust, understanding, and authenticity.

Chapter 2: Crafting an Irresistible Customer Experience

2.1 Elements of a Memorable Customer Experience

In the business world, success hinges on the ability to captivate customers, not just for a single transaction but for a lasting, mutually beneficial relationship. Crafting an irresistible customer experience is the linchpin of this endeavor. Let's delve into the foundational elements that shape a memorable customer experience.

Ease of Purchase and User-Friendly Interfaces

The customer experience starts well before a purchase is made – it begins with the very first interaction, and one of the most pivotal aspects of this interaction is the ease of purchase. It's a simple yet often underestimated factor. In the digital age, this translates to your website or app. Think of it as the front door of your business. When a customer lands on your site, they should find it not just navigable, but inviting and intuitive.

A user-friendly interface is one that minimizes confusion and friction. Buttons, links, and menus are clear and well-organized. The path to purchase is obvious, and shopping carts are easy to access and edit. Payment options are varied and secure. This simplicity creates an environment where customers can quickly find what they need, make informed choices, and complete a purchase hassle-free.

Businesses must ensure that their customers can seamlessly find, select, and acquire their products or services. Here's how you can make this happen:

Simplicity is Key: The golden rule here is simplicity. A cluttered, complex, or confusing buying process is a surefire way to drive potential customers away. Your website or storefront should be clean and uncluttered, with an intuitive navigation structure. Shoppers should know where they are, how to find what they want, and how to complete a purchase, all without a second thought.

Streamlined Checkout: Have you ever abandoned an online shopping cart because the checkout process seemed to require your life story and a degree in computer science to complete? Well, your customers feel the same way. A streamlined checkout process with minimal, necessary steps is vital. Offer guest checkout options and secure payment gateways to boost customer confidence.

Mobile Optimization: The modern customer is on the move, often shopping from their smartphones. It's imperative to ensure that your online interfaces are fully responsive and mobile-optimized. The ease of mobile browsing and purchasing cannot be underestimated, and a poor mobile experience can deter even the most interested customers.

Consider the online retail giant, Amazon. Their site is a model of ease and efficiency. It anticipates your needs, offers personalized recommendations, and ensures the buying process is a breeze. Amazon is like the superstore of the internet, but its layout is designed to make sure customers don't feel overwhelmed by choice. It's no surprise that their user-friendly interface has played a significant role in their customer satisfaction and loyalty.

Seamless Customer Service and Support

A seamless customer service experience is the backbone of any business's success. It's not just about addressing issues when they arise – it's about proactively engaging with customers to understand their needs and provide support when required. It's also about consistency. Customers should receive the same level of support whether they're reaching out via email, chat, phone, or social media.

When a customer has questions or faces issues, how you respond can make or break their perception of your brand. Here's how to create a seamless support system:

Prompt Responsiveness: In today's world of instant messaging and rapid responses, waiting for a reply feels like an eternity. Ensure that your customer support team is agile and responsive. Your customers should feel heard and valued, and their queries should be addressed promptly, whether through live chat, email, or phone.

Omnichannel Support: It's not enough to offer support through a single channel. Your customers may prefer different modes of communication. Provide options like live chat, email, social media, and phone support. Crucially, maintain consistency in information and service quality across all channels.

Empowered Support Staff: Equip your customer support team with the tools and authority to resolve issues swiftly. A well-empowered support agent can turn a potentially negative experience into a positive one. Trust your team to make the right decisions when addressing customer concerns.

A stellar example of this is Zappos. Their legendary customer service is characterized by a willingness to go above and beyond. They don't just answer customer inquiries; they create a memorable experience through genuine, friendly interactions. Customers remember Zappos not just for their shoes but for the impeccable service that accompanies them.

The Art of Exceeding Customer Expectations

To truly craft an irresistible customer experience, you must master the art of exceeding customer expectations. This is the secret sauce that transforms satisfied customers into loyal advocates. Here's how to go above and beyond:

Underpromise and Overdeliver: One of the most effective ways to exceed expectations is to underpromise and overdeliver. Set realistic expectations for your customers, and then surpass them. If you promise a product delivery in seven days and it arrives in five, you've just created a pleasant surprise.

Personalization with Precision: Personalization goes beyond addressing customers by their first name in an email. It involves understanding their preferences, habits, and purchase history. Use this information to recommend products or services that are genuinely relevant to them. When customers feel that you "get" them, they're more likely to stay.

Surprise and Delight: Infuse unexpected moments of delight into your customer experience. It could be a handwritten thank-you note in a shipped package, a small surprise discount, or a birthday gift. These unexpected gestures create emotional connections and leave lasting impressions.

Let's break it down further. Picture a situation where a customer orders a product for express shipping. You not only ensure the product arrives ahead of schedule but also include a handwritten thank-you note and a small, unexpected gift as a token of appreciation. The impact of this exceeds mere customer satisfaction; it fosters customer loyalty.

One of the prime examples of this approach is Disney. The company is renowned for its unwavering commitment to exceeding customer expectations. Their entire business model is built around creating magical experiences. Whether it's a surprise character appearance in the park, personalized messages from beloved Disney characters, or an unexpected upgrade during a stay at a Disney resort, they understand the art of exceeding expectations.

Crafting an irresistible customer experience isn't about empty promises or flashy marketing. It's about the nitty-gritty details of making the customer's interaction with your business smooth, enjoyable, and memorable. Ease of purchase, seamless support, and exceeding expectations form the bedrock of a customer experience that's not just irresistible but unforgettable. When you master these elements, you're well on your way to creating loyal customers who not only come back for more but also advocate for your brand to others.

2.2 Going Beyond Transactions

In today's fiercely competitive business landscape, simply conducting transactions is no longer enough to win the hearts and wallets of your customers. To create an irresistible customer experience, we must delve deeper, reaching out to customers on a personal level, making them feel valued, and forging lasting connections. In this section, we explore three vital aspects of transcending mere transactions: Building Customer Loyalty through Personalization, The Role of Storytelling in Customer Engagement, and Using Moments of Delight to Create Lasting Impressions.

Building Customer Loyalty through Personalization

In a world overflowing with choices, customers have come to expect more than a one-size-fits-all approach. To truly captivate them, personalization is the key. This isn't just about using their first name in an email; it's about understanding their preferences, needs, and habits. It's about showing them that you see and appreciate their individuality.

Personalization starts with data. Your customers generate a wealth of information with every interaction - from their purchase history to their online behavior. Harness this data to create tailored experiences. If a customer is a frequent visitor to your coffee shop and consistently orders a caramel macchiato, why not offer them a personalized loyalty program centered around their favorite drink? It's about making them feel special, like you're attuned to their needs.

Additionally, personalization extends to the content you deliver. It's about providing product recommendations that resonate with their interests, sending targeted promotions, and tailoring your communication to align with their preferences. Whether it's through email marketing, product suggestions, or user experiences on your website, personalization enhances the sense of individual attention. When a customer receives recommendations that match their taste, they feel understood, fostering a deeper connection with your brand.

The Role of Storytelling in Customer Engagement
Facts and figures might inform, but stories resonate. People remember stories because they elicit emotions and connect with the human experience. This is why storytelling plays an integral role in crafting an irresistible customer experience. Stories provide context, evoking empathy, and allowing customers to relate on a personal level.

When you tell your brand's story, it should go beyond mere marketing rhetoric. It should reflect your values, your journey, and the impact you've made on your customers' lives. Share customer success stories that illustrate the transformation your products or services have brought about. These tales of real people with real challenges who found solutions through your offerings create a powerful connection.

Furthermore, storytelling extends beyond your brand's narrative. Encourage your customers to share their stories too. Create platforms for them to tell their tales of success or the meaningful moments they've experienced with your products. Testimonials, reviews, and user-generated content all contribute to the narrative of your brand. They become part of your brand's story.

Effective storytelling is not about embellishment or fiction; it's about authenticity. Share your struggles and the lessons you've learned. Highlight the challenges your customers faced and how they overcame them. These narratives engender trust and authenticity, making your brand more relatable. They provide an emotional anchor, grounding the customer in a shared journey.

Using Moments of Delight to Create Lasting Impressions

In the pursuit of crafting an irresistible customer experience, it's the little things that matter. Moments of delight are those unexpected, thoughtful touches that elevate an ordinary transaction into an unforgettable encounter. These moments linger in the minds of your customers and reinforce the emotional connection they have with your brand.

Think of moments of delight as surprises that go beyond what's expected. It could be as simple as a handwritten thank-you note in the package when they receive their order, or a personalized video message expressing your appreciation for their loyalty. These gestures communicate that you value them, not just their business.

Moreover, moments of delight can take the form of unexpected perks. Offer exclusive discounts, access to pre-sales, or loyalty rewards that demonstrate a commitment to making their experience special. Create a sense of anticipation and excitement by announcing limited-time offers or special events.

Moments of delight don't always have to be related to promotions; they can also involve exceptional customer service. Train your staff to actively listen and empathize with customers. When a customer faces a challenge or has a unique request, an empathetic response can turn a potentially negative experience into a memorable one.

The key is to surprise and delight without being contrived. Authenticity matters. Moments of delight should be driven by a genuine desire to make your customers' lives better, not just to sell more. When customers experience these moments, they're more likely to become your brand's advocates, sharing their positive encounters with others.

Moving beyond transactions to create an irresistible customer experience involves a strategic blend of personalization, storytelling, and moments of delight. These elements add depth and authenticity to your interactions, forging stronger connections and turning customers into loyal advocates. By implementing these practices, you can establish a brand that resonates on a personal level, fostering lasting relationships with your customers and driving business growth.

2.3 Measuring and Improving the Customer Experience

In the realm of business, knowledge is power. If you aim to craft an irresistible customer experience, you must first understand how your customers perceive your brand. In this section, we dive into the art of measuring and improving the customer experience, a crucial aspect of the ever-evolving business landscape.

Key Metrics for Evaluating Customer Satisfaction

In our way to create an irresistible customer experience, your experience begins with measurement. Metrics are your compass, guiding you through the uncharted waters of customer satisfaction. To navigate effectively, you must first understand the key metrics that evaluate customer contentment.

* Net Promoter Score (NPS): A simple yet powerful metric that gauges customer loyalty. NPS asks a fundamental question: "On a scale of 0 to 10, how likely are you to recommend our product or service to a friend?" It segregates your customers into Promoters (9-10), Passives (7-8), and Detractors (0-6). Your goal? Maximize Promoters and minimize Detractors.

* Customer Satisfaction Score (CSAT): This metric is all about the here and now. It asks customers to rate their satisfaction with a recent interaction, typically on a scale from 1 to 5 or 1 to 7. It's a quick pulse-check to evaluate your performance on a transactional level.

* Customer Effort Score (CES): This metric focuses on the ease with which customers can resolve issues or complete tasks. It's often measured through surveys asking customers how easy or difficult it was to achieve their goal.

* Churn Rate: The percentage of customers who cut ties with your brand during a specific time period. If your churn rate is high, it's a glaring sign that you're not meeting customer expectations.

* Customer Retention Rate: The flip side of churn. It tells you how many customers stick around. A high retention rate indicates satisfied customers who keep coming back for more.

* First Response Time (FRT): In the digital age, prompt responses matter. FRT measures how quickly your team reacts to customer inquiries. A swift response time can

make the difference between a satisfied customer and one who jumps ship.

* Customer Lifetime Value (CLV): A long-term perspective on customer worth. CLV calculates the total revenue you can expect from a single customer throughout their relationship with your brand. A higher CLV indicates loyal, satisfied customers who continually engage with your business.

Gathering and Analyzing Customer Feedback
Now that you're equipped with the compass of metrics, it's time to gather insights directly from the source: your customers. Feedback is a priceless asset, providing you with unfiltered glimpses into their minds.

Customer Surveys: Surveys are your best friends in the realm of feedback. They can be deployed through email, on your website, or via mobile apps. Keep questions clear, concise, and relevant. Ask about their experience, what they liked, what they didn't, and their suggestions for improvement.

Customer Interviews: Face-to-face or over the phone, interviews allow for in-depth discussions. Ask open-ended questions and let your customers share their experiences and emotions. This qualitative data is invaluable for understanding the 'why' behind the 'what.'

Social Media Monitoring: Social platforms are a treasure trove of unsolicited feedback. Monitor mentions, comments, and messages. Respond promptly, showing your commitment to addressing concerns and appreciating positive feedback.

Online Reviews: Review platforms like Yelp, TripAdvisor, and Google Reviews are real-time indicators of customer sentiment. Encourage satisfied customers to leave positive reviews, and proactively address negative ones. Publicly demonstrating your dedication to customer satisfaction can turn detractors into promoters.

Implementing Changes for Continuous Improvement

With metrics in hand and feedback analyzed, the next step is the key to crafting an irresistible customer experience—implementation. There's no magic formula for success, but there are clear steps you can take to drive improvements.

Identify Pain Points: Metrics and feedback often highlight areas where customers experience dissatisfaction or inconvenience. These are your pain points. Whether it's a clunky checkout process, long response times, or confusing navigation, pinpoint the pain points.

Set Clear Objectives: Once you've identified the issues, set clear and specific objectives for improvement. For example, if customers complain about slow response times, your objective might be to reduce the first response time by 50%.

Engage Your Team: Your team is the engine behind these improvements. Get them on board by sharing the objectives, the metrics, and the feedback. Encourage their input and ideas. They're the ones who will make it happen.

Implement Changes Incrementally: Rome wasn't built in a day, and neither are extraordinary customer experiences. Make gradual changes, continually monitoring metrics to see if you're moving the needle.

Measure the Impact: As you implement changes, keep a close eye on how they impact your metrics. Is your NPS score rising? Is FRT decreasing? Are more customers turning from Detractors to Promoters? Use this data to fine-tune your approach.

Incorporate Feedback Loops: Customer feedback should be a continuous process. Implement feedback loops that allow you to stay in touch with your customers, solicit their input, and keep refining your experience.

Remember, creating an irresistible customer experience is an ongoing process. It's about constantly striving to meet and exceed customer expectations. As you measure, gather feedback, and implement improvements, you'll be well on your way to crafting an experience that keeps customers coming back for more.

Chapter 3: Loyalty Programs and Customer Incentives

3.1 The Science of Loyalty Programs

In a world teeming with choices and competition, businesses are constantly seeking the holy grail of customer loyalty. They want customers not just to make a purchase but to keep coming back, to choose them over the sea of alternatives. The question is, how can businesses effectively nurture this allegiance, turning sporadic buyers into devoted patrons? The answer lies in the systematic and strategic world of loyalty programs and customer incentives.

Types of Loyalty Programs

Loyalty programs come in various forms and flavors, but they all share a common goal: to keep customers engaged and committed. To understand the science behind these programs, we must first dissect the different types that exist.

* Points-Based Programs: Perhaps the most familiar, these programs reward customers with points for each purchase. Over time, these points accumulate and can be redeemed for discounts, free products, or other incentives. Points-based programs create a sense of achievement and a tangible path toward a reward.

* Tiered Loyalty Programs: Tiered systems are like the modern-day version of a meritocracy. Customers ascend through different tiers or levels, each offering increasing

benefits. The higher the tier, the more exclusive and valuable the rewards. This structure encourages customers to not only stay but to spend more to attain the next tier.

* Punch Cards and Frequency Programs: Simple yet effective, these programs rely on the basic principle of accumulation. For every purchase, customers receive a 'punch' or a stamp on their loyalty card. Once the card is complete, they're rewarded with a free item or discount. The psychology here is about creating a sense of progress and a visual representation of rewards to come.

* Subscription-Based Loyalty: Subscription programs offer customers exclusive perks, often in the form of early access, special promotions, or unique content. They engage customers by providing ongoing value in exchange for a regular fee, fostering a sense of belonging to an elite club.

The Psychology of Rewards and Incentives
The foundation of loyalty programs lies in the intricate world of human psychology. Rewards and incentives tap into our innate desires and tendencies. They trigger specific emotions and behaviors that businesses can harness to build strong, lasting connections.

* The Pleasure of Accumulation: Points-based systems and punch cards are grounded in the joy of collecting. Each point earned creates a sense of accomplishment, akin to leveling up in a video game. It triggers the brain's pleasure centers, fostering the desire to keep collecting and spending.

* The Fear of Missing Out: Tiered loyalty programs play on the potent emotion of 'FOMO'—the fear of missing out. When customers see the benefits of the next tier, they're compelled to reach it, lest they miss out on exclusive rewards. It's a psychological push that keeps them engaged and spending.

* Reciprocity and Gratitude: When customers receive rewards, they feel a sense of gratitude. In psychological terms, this is known as 'reciprocity.' People inherently want to return a favor or kindness. When customers are given something, they're more inclined to reciprocate with continued loyalty and spending.

* Instant Gratification: In a world where we can have almost anything at our fingertips with a few clicks, instant gratification is a powerful motivator. Loyalty programs that offer immediate discounts, freebies, or exclusive access leverage this human desire for quick rewards.

Building Customer Affinity through Loyalty
The ultimate aim of any loyalty program isn't just to reward purchases but to build customer affinity. Loyalty programs should transform customers into loyal advocates who feel a deep connection with the brand. Here's how the science of loyalty programs achieves this:

* Enhanced Customer Experience: Loyalty programs often come with perks like faster customer support, priority service, or exclusive access. These benefits elevate the

customer experience and create an emotional attachment to the brand.

* Emotional Bonds: Rewards and incentives aren't just transactional; they're emotional triggers. Customers who receive personalized discounts, surprise gifts, or exclusive offers feel a sense of appreciation and emotional connection to the brand.

* Community and Social Proof: Some loyalty programs foster a sense of community among members. For example, Starbucks' loyalty program isn't just about free coffee; it's about being part of the Starbucks community. When customers feel they belong, they're more likely to advocate for the brand among their peers.

Loyalty programs are not just about discounts and rewards. They're about understanding the psychology of your customers and using that knowledge to foster deep connections. When executed effectively, they can transform ordinary buyers into passionate advocates who keep coming back, not just for the perks but for the emotional bond they share with your brand.

3.2 Gamification and Customer Engagement

In the world of business, loyalty is gold. Every loyal customer is like a precious gem in your treasure chest, contributing not only to your revenue but also to the longevity and prosperity of your enterprise. However, loyalty is not bestowed; it's earned. This is where loyalty programs come into play, and within these programs lies a sparkling jewel of customer engagement – gamification.

Gamification Elements in Loyalty Programs

Let's start by breaking down the elements of gamification within loyalty programs. Gamification is the art of taking game-like elements and incorporating them into your business processes, and it's not just about turning your business into a game. It's about understanding the psychology of motivation, rewards, and competition.

Points and Rewards: Imagine your loyalty program as a game board. Your customers accumulate points for every action they take, like making a purchase, referring a friend, or writing a product review. These points aren't just numbers; they're badges of honor, tokens of achievement. The more points they earn, the closer they get to unlocking rewards, whether it's a discount, a free product, or exclusive access.

Challenges and Achievements: Just like in a video game where players complete missions to advance, your customers can take on challenges. Completing these challenges gives them a sense of accomplishment and motivates them to keep engaging with your brand. The achievement badges they earn are like digital trophies that they proudly display.

Leaderboards: Competition is a powerful motivator. Leaderboards show your customers where they stand in relation to others. It's the race to the top. When customers see their names climbing higher on that list, it fuels their determination and engagement.

Status Levels: Humans crave recognition and status. Gamified loyalty programs often have tiered levels, like bronze, silver, and gold. These levels create a sense of belonging and hierarchy. Customers strive to ascend the ranks, aiming for that prestigious gold level. It's not just about the rewards; it's about the status that comes with it.

Creating Fun and Engaging Customer Experiences
Now that we've dissected the elements, let's delve into the heart of gamification – creating fun and engaging customer experiences. Your loyalty program shouldn't be a mundane list of tasks and rewards. It should be a journey filled with excitement and anticipation.

Unlocking Mystery: Humans are curious creatures. The element of surprise can be thrilling. In your loyalty program, incorporate surprise rewards, bonus challenges, or hidden treasures. Your customers will keep coming back to uncover the next surprise, and every surprise encountered becomes a memorable experience.

Storytelling: Imagine your loyalty program as a story – your customers are the heroes. Weaving a narrative into your program adds depth and resonance. Each action they take, each reward they earn, contributes to their own unique storyline. It's a tale of their triumphs and their loyalty to your brand.

Personalization: Tailoring the experience to the individual is the heart of customer engagement. Your customers aren't just part of a program; they are unique individuals. Recognize their preferences, their history with your brand, and customize challenges and rewards accordingly. The more personalized the experience, the stronger the connection.

Inclusivity: Gamification isn't just for the gamers. Make it accessible and enjoyable for everyone. It should be simple to understand and participate in. The more inclusive your program is, the broader your audience becomes.

Case Studies of Successful Gamified Loyalty Programs

Now, let's paint a vivid picture with case studies of successful gamified loyalty programs. These stories show how gamification can turn casual customers into enthusiastic brand advocates.

Starbucks Rewards: Picture a world where your morning coffee becomes a game. Starbucks Rewards introduced a tiered system, making customers feel like they're leveling up in a coffee-loving RPG. The excitement of reaching Gold status, coupled with personalized drink recommendations and early access to new products, turns each visit to Starbucks into an adventure.

Sephora Beauty Insider: Sephora transformed makeup shopping into a beauty journey. With their gamified Beauty Insider program, customers unlock rewards, gain access to exclusive events, and receive birthday gifts. The result? A loyal community of beauty enthusiasts who love to share their favorite products and techniques.

Nike Training Club: Nike's gamified fitness app encourages users to stay active by offering rewards like exclusive workouts and gear discounts. Users set personal fitness goals and track their progress, feeling a sense of accomplishment and belonging to the Nike fitness community.

In the realm of loyalty programs and gamification, success stories are abundant, and these are just a few gems. The common thread among them is the ability to make customers feel special, recognized, and motivated to return. When you gamify your loyalty program, you're not just rewarding your customers; you're creating an experience that keeps them engaged and eager to continue their journey with your brand. Gamification isn't just a gimmick; it's a powerful tool that can turn loyal customers into your most vocal and dedicated sales force.

3.3 Beyond Discounts: Creative Incentives

In today's fiercely competitive business landscape, attracting and retaining loyal customers is an art form that demands innovation and a keen understanding of what truly motivates individuals. Loyalty programs are a time-tested strategy that has proven its worth, but the key lies in going beyond the ordinary, beyond the mundane discounts, to offer creative incentives that not only capture your customers' attention but keep them coming back for more. In this section, we will delve into the realm of non-monetary incentives and recognition, experiential rewards, and exclusive access, all while maintaining a critical eye on the balance between costs and benefits.

Non-Monetary Incentives and Recognition

Imagine a loyal customer walking into your store, not just expecting the usual run-of-the-mill discount but looking forward to an experience that transcends mere transactional savings. Non-monetary incentives and recognition are a powerful tool in your arsenal. Why? Because they tap into the human desire for acknowledgment and appreciation.

Recognition can take many forms. It can be as simple as a personalized thank-you note or as grand as a dedicated customer appreciation event. The key is to make your customers feel special, acknowledged, and appreciated.

Non-monetary incentives go beyond the traditional loyalty program rewards. They're about acknowledging your customers' loyalty in a way that touches their hearts. Consider offering exclusive access to sneak previews of new products, personalized recommendations, or access to a loyalty club with benefits like early access to sales. These incentives make your customers feel valued and recognized, building a genuine emotional connection to your brand.

Experiential Rewards and Exclusive Access

Discounts are a tried-and-true method to drive customer loyalty, but experiential rewards and exclusive access take it a step further. They elevate the customer experience to an entirely new level. Experiences are something that money can't always buy, and it's the rarity and exclusivity of these rewards that make them truly compelling.

Imagine a customer who's been with your business for years. Instead of another coupon code, they receive an invitation to an exclusive behind-the-scenes tour of your manufacturing facility. They get a chance to witness the magic behind your products, meet the team, and even have a hands-on experience. That's the kind of reward that leaves an indelible mark on the customer's memory.

Exclusivity is a driving force here. By granting access to experiences that are not available to the general public, you're fostering a sense of belonging, a VIP status that customers will strive to maintain. This exclusivity can manifest in many forms – from private shopping events and limited-edition products to exclusive webinars and workshops.

The psychology behind experiential rewards is intriguing. When customers receive a tangible item, like a discount code, it's easy to forget. But experiences create lasting memories. The emotional impact lingers long after the event, and those positive feelings are associated with your brand.

Balancing Costs and Benefits of Loyalty Programs

While the allure of creative incentives is undeniable, it's crucial to balance the costs and benefits of loyalty programs. You may be wondering, "Are these innovative incentives worth the investment?" The answer is a resounding "yes," but with a caveat.

Creative incentives, especially experiential ones, may have a higher upfront cost than traditional discounts. However, they often yield a higher return on investment in the long run. Experiences and exclusivity can create a buzz around your brand, increase customer lifetime value, and encourage word-of-mouth marketing.

To strike the right balance, it's imperative to measure and track the impact of your loyalty programs. Understand the costs involved and the benefits they bring. Collect data, measure customer retention rates, and calculate the revenue generated from loyal customers. This data will provide a clear picture of the return on investment.

Furthermore, consider tiered loyalty programs. By offering different levels of rewards and experiences based on customer loyalty, you can ensure that the costs align with the benefits. New customers may receive a warm welcome and introductory discounts, while long-term loyal customers enjoy the full spectrum of creative incentives.

Loyalty programs have evolved far beyond the realm of mere discounts. They have transformed into a means of fostering emotional connections and creating lasting memories. Non-monetary incentives, recognition, experiential rewards, and exclusive access are the cornerstones of these new-age loyalty programs. They not only attract and retain loyal customers but also turn them into passionate advocates for your brand.

The balance between costs and benefits is crucial. While creative incentives may seem more expensive upfront, their long-term impact can be profound. By measuring the return on investment and tailoring programs to different customer segments, you can ensure that your loyalty programs are not just a cost but a strategic investment that pays rich dividends in the form of customer loyalty and advocacy.

In the end, it's not just about discounts; it's about creating experiences and connections that resonate with your customers on a personal level. These are the strategies that transform loyal customers into devoted brand ambassadors, propelling your business to new heights.

Chapter 4: Personalized Marketing and Communication

4.1 The Art of Personalization

In the landscape of modern business, the art of personalization has emerged as a cornerstone of success. It's a game-changer, a dynamic force that has revolutionized the way we engage with customers. The days of generic, one-size-fits-all marketing messages are long gone. In this section, we delve into the intricate world of personalization, dissecting its core elements, and unveiling its transformative potential.

Personalizing Marketing Messages

Picture this: you receive an email from your favorite online retailer, and it's not just another generic message. It begins with your name, and the subject line hints at products you've recently browsed. As you open the email, you find tailored recommendations, exclusive discounts, and content that aligns perfectly with your interests. It's as if the message was crafted just for you, and that's precisely what personalization in marketing achieves.

Personalizing marketing messages isn't merely about inserting a recipient's name into an email. It's about understanding your customers on a profound level. It involves scrutinizing their past behaviors, preferences, and purchase history. Armed with this knowledge, you can create messages that resonate with them personally, forging a deeper connection.

This personalized approach extends beyond email marketing. It includes tailoring social media posts, advertisements, and even the content on your website to match each visitor's unique interests. The aim is to make customers feel seen and valued, as if you have taken the time to understand their individual needs.

But why is this so crucial in the grand scheme of things? The answer lies in the psychology of human behavior. We, as individuals, are naturally drawn to experiences that make us feel special. When a marketing message speaks directly to our desires and interests, it captures our attention. It's no longer noise in the background; it becomes a relevant and meaningful part of our lives.

When you personalize your marketing messages, it's not just about the data you collect; it's about the value you deliver. Here are a few key points to consider:

Understanding Your Customers: To personalize effectively, you need to understand your customers inside out. Analyze their purchase history, their browsing behavior on your website, and any other touchpoints they have with your brand. What are their preferences, and what motivates them to make a purchase?

Segmentation and Targeting: Once you have a wealth of data, the next step is segmentation. You group customers with similar characteristics, preferences, and behaviors together. This allows you to create tailored messages for each segment.

Crafting Personalized Messages: Personalized marketing messages involve more than just inserting a customer's name into an email. It's about crafting content that speaks directly to their needs and desires. If a customer has shown an interest in a specific product category, your message should focus on that category, highlighting new arrivals, recommendations, or exclusive offers.

Timing Matters: The timing of your messages can be just as crucial as the content. Sending a message at the right moment, such as a special offer on a product they've been eyeing, can significantly increase conversion rates.

Feedback Loop: Personalization is not static; it's an ongoing process. Encourage customers to provide feedback and preferences, and make sure you listen and respond. This not only enhances the personalization but also fosters a sense of being heard and valued.

By personalizing your marketing messages, you're not just targeting a mass of potential customers; you're speaking to each individual personally, acknowledging their unique needs and desires. This approach fosters a sense of trust and authenticity in your brand, and it's a surefire way to stand out in today's crowded marketplace.

Dynamic Content and Targeted Campaigns
To grasp the art of personalization fully, one must understand the significance of dynamic content and targeted campaigns. These are the tools that breathe life

into personalized marketing, enabling you to connect with your audience on a profound level.

Dynamic content is a game-changer in the world of personalization. It involves creating marketing materials that adapt in real-time to the individual preferences of each recipient. Imagine a scenario where your website showcases different products to different visitors based on their past interactions. Or an email that changes its content depending on the recipient's location or recent browsing behavior. This isn't science fiction; it's dynamic content in action.

Dynamic content is the embodiment of personalized marketing. It allows you to deliver a unique experience to every customer, ensuring that what they see and interact with is precisely what they're looking for. It's not just about showing the right products; it's about telling a story that resonates with each customer, fostering a connection that goes beyond the transaction.

And then there are targeted campaigns, the tactical side of personalization. These campaigns are meticulously designed to appeal to specific segments of your audience. By creating campaigns that address the specific needs and pain points of different customer groups, you can speak directly to their concerns, making your marketing more relevant and persuasive.

Take, for example, a clothing retailer launching a targeted campaign for winter apparel. This campaign is sent to customers who reside in colder regions, while a separate campaign promoting summer wear goes out to those in warmer areas. It's not only about showing the right products; it's about speaking to the seasonal realities of each group, making the marketing message resonate.

Consider a scenario where an e-commerce website showcases different products to different users based on their past behavior. If User A frequently browses athletic shoes, the homepage will prominently display the latest running shoe arrivals, whereas User B, who leans towards fashion accessories, will see an array of designer handbags. This level of customization captures the essence of dynamic content.

Tailored Recommendations: Dynamic content allows you to provide tailored product recommendations based on a customer's browsing and purchase history. Recommendations may vary from "Customers who bought this also bought" to "Inspired by your recent purchase."

Content Personalization: Beyond product recommendations, dynamic content applies to all types of content, including blog posts, articles, or news updates. Users with different interests see content relevant to their preferences.

Email Marketing: Dynamic content is particularly impactful in email marketing. With dynamic emails, you can send a single email campaign to a large list, but the content within the email changes to suit each recipient. This method enables you to send personalized offers, product updates, or news, all in one email.

Targeted Campaigns: Rather than sending a generic message to your entire customer base, you can create targeted campaigns that address specific segments of your audience. For example, a fashion retailer might create a campaign for a new clothing line and send it to customers who have previously shown an interest in similar items.

Real-Time Personalization: Thanks to modern data analytics, you can now personalize content in real-time. When a customer visits your website, the content and offers they see can adjust instantly based on their actions and preferences.

By harnessing dynamic content and targeted campaigns, you're placing your marketing in a class of its own. You're sending a message to your customers that you're not just interested in making a sale; you're genuinely concerned about their needs and preferences. And in a world bombarded by generic marketing noise, this is a breath of fresh air.

Benefits of Personalization for Customers

The benefits of personalization in marketing are twofold – they extend to both your business and your customers. While your business reaps the rewards of increased engagement, conversions, and customer loyalty, your customers experience a range of advantages that enhance their overall satisfaction and shopping experience.

For customers, personalization translates into an enhanced shopping experience. It means that they are more likely to discover products that align with their preferences, leading to a sense of efficiency and convenience. Imagine logging into your favorite e-commerce platform, and the homepage is adorned with products that genuinely resonate with your tastes. It's like having your own personal shopper, available around the clock.

Personalization also has a profound impact on customer retention. When customers feel understood and valued, they are more likely to return to your brand. Loyalty is cultivated through personalized experiences that demonstrate an understanding of individual preferences and a commitment to making their lives easier.

But it doesn't stop there. Personalization also empowers customers with relevant recommendations and insights, helping them make more informed decisions. When they receive product suggestions based on their past purchases or browsing behavior, they are more likely to explore and discover items they might not have considered otherwise. It's a win-win; the customer finds new products, and your business increases sales.

Moreover, personalization offers customers a sense of control. When they can customize their experiences and see content and products tailored to their interests, they feel as though they are in the driver's seat. This leads to increased customer satisfaction and trust in your brand.

Personalization is not merely a trend; it's a fundamental shift in how businesses engage with customers. It's a strategy that transcends the traditional, one-size-fits-all approach to marketing, providing a deeper, more personal connection with your audience. By personalizing marketing messages, employing dynamic content, and creating targeted campaigns, you're not only enhancing your business's bottom line but also improving the lives of your customers. It's a transformative art that distinguishes you in a competitive marketplace and forges lasting relationships.

4.2 Leveraging Data for Personalization

In the modern business landscape, where customers have a multitude of options at their fingertips, personalization has become a paramount strategy. It's the art of making each customer feel like they're not just another face in the crowd but an individual whose needs and preferences are genuinely understood. Achieving this level of personalization requires a data-driven approach, which is precisely what we'll explore in this section.

Collecting and Analyzing Customer Data

Effective personalization begins with collecting and analyzing customer data. To provide a personalized experience, businesses need to understand their customers on a deeper level. This involves gathering data from various sources, such as website interactions, purchase history, and even customer feedback.

Customer data is the foundation upon which personalized marketing is built. By harnessing data, businesses can gain valuable insights into their customers' behavior and preferences. This data can be as basic as demographic information, like age and location, or as intricate as tracking a customer's online journey, understanding what they clicked on, what they purchased, and what they abandoned in their cart.

The magic lies in the analysis of this data. Sophisticated tools and algorithms help businesses discern patterns and trends, allowing them to make predictions about what customers might be interested in next. This empowers businesses to not only meet the current needs of their customers but also anticipate their future desires.

Take, for example, an e-commerce website. By analyzing a customer's past purchase history, their search queries, and their browsing behavior, the platform can suggest products that align with their interests. If a customer recently purchased hiking gear and frequently reads about outdoor adventures, the system may suggest camping equipment or rugged footwear. This level of personalized product recommendation is only made possible through effective data collection and analysis.

However, a word of caution is essential when collecting and handling customer data: privacy and ethics must be paramount. It's imperative to be transparent about data collection practices, provide opt-in options, and ensure that data is securely stored. Customer trust is fragile, and mishandling data can lead to severe consequences.

Predictive Analytics and Customer Behavior

Predictive analytics is a pivotal tool in the realm of personalization. It involves using historical customer data and patterns to predict future behavior. By recognizing these trends, businesses can tailor their marketing efforts to cater to individual preferences and needs.

Imagine a scenario where an online bookstore seeks to personalize the recommendations for its customers. By analyzing a customer's previous book purchases, the genres they prefer, and the authors they admire, predictive analytics can suggest books that align with the customer's literary taste. This not only enhances the customer's shopping experience but also increases the likelihood of additional purchases.

Moreover, predictive analytics is not confined to just product recommendations. It can also be used to forecast customer churn. By identifying patterns that indicate a customer might be dissatisfied or disengaged, businesses can intervene proactively, offering solutions or incentives to retain their valuable patrons.

The beauty of predictive analytics is its adaptability. It evolves as more data is collected, becoming increasingly accurate and refined. It's akin to having a crystal ball, allowing businesses to anticipate customer needs and tailor their marketing strategies with precision.

Privacy and Ethical Considerations in Data Usage

While the potential of data-driven personalization is vast, it should always be pursued with a strong ethical compass and a profound respect for customer privacy. In an age where data breaches and privacy concerns make headlines, trust is fragile, and maintaining it is paramount.

Respecting customer privacy begins with transparency. Customers should be informed about what data is being collected, how it will be used, and given the option to opt out if they so choose. Consent is the cornerstone of ethical data usage.

Moreover, data should be protected rigorously. Cybersecurity is non-negotiable. The consequences of a data breach can be severe, both in terms of financial loss and damage to reputation. Customers must have confidence that their data is safe in your hands.

Data should be used for the benefit of the customer, not solely for the gain of the business. The goal should be to enhance the customer's experience, not to manipulate or exploit them. Honesty and integrity should guide every data-driven decision.

It's essential to comply with data protection regulations and laws applicable in your region. Legal requirements vary, but many have stringent rules on how data is collected and used. Non-compliance can lead to heavy fines and significant reputational damage.

Personalized marketing through data analysis is a powerful tool, but it must be wielded with care and respect.

Customers are willing to share their data when they trust that it will be used to enhance their experience. Therefore, the responsible collection, analysis, and application of customer data should always be guided by transparency, security, and ethical considerations. It's not just about increasing sales; it's about nurturing lasting customer relationships built on trust and respect.

4.3 Omni-Channel Marketing

In today's hyper-connected world, marketing is no longer confined to a single channel. Customers now interact with brands through various touchpoints, both online and offline. This shift has given rise to the concept of Omni-Channel Marketing, a strategy that seeks to create a seamless, integrated customer experience. Let's delve into this crucial section and explore how Omni-Channel Marketing can transform your business by connecting your online and offline efforts.

Seamless Cross-Channel Customer Experience

Omni-Channel Marketing is all about creating a consistent and seamless experience for your customers, regardless of where they interact with your brand. It's about recognizing that modern consumers don't distinguish between your online and offline presence. To them, it's all one entity – your brand.

Imagine a scenario where a customer first comes across your brand's social media ad while scrolling through their newsfeed on their smartphone. They click on the ad, explore your website, and even add a few items to their online shopping cart. Later, they decide to visit a physical store. In an ideal Omni-Channel experience, their interactions would seamlessly transition. They might receive a personalized discount on their mobile as they enter the store, guiding them to those items they liked online.

Creating such a seamless transition requires a deep understanding of your customers, their preferences, and their behaviors across all touchpoints. It involves leveraging data analytics to track customer interactions, collect feedback, and identify pain points in their journey. By removing friction and providing consistent experiences, you can create a bond of trust with your customers that transcends channels.

Integrating Online and Offline Marketing Efforts
Omni-Channel Marketing is the bridge between your digital and physical marketing strategies. It's the art of connecting the dots and ensuring that your customers' experiences remain consistent and complementary across all touchpoints.

Consider a scenario where you operate an e-commerce store and a brick-and-mortar retail location. Your customers may visit your physical store to explore products and then decide to make a purchase online. To integrate these experiences effectively, you could offer in-store kiosks where customers can place online orders, providing the convenience of choice while reinforcing the idea that the online and offline channels are interconnected.

Moreover, Omni-Channel Marketing involves harmonizing the messaging and branding between these channels. Your in-store signage, your website, and your social media profiles should all convey a consistent message. It's about making sure that your customers recognize your brand no matter where they encounter it.

The beauty of integration is that it doesn't merely connect channels; it also bridges the gap between the online and offline worlds. By doing so, you empower your customers to interact with your brand in the way that suits them best, and that's a powerful way to build loyalty.

Measuring the Impact of Omni-Channel Strategies
In the world of marketing, measurement is key. You need to know whether your efforts are paying off and, more importantly, how you can improve. Omni-Channel Marketing is no exception, and tracking its impact is crucial to its success.

Start by setting clear, measurable objectives. These objectives should be tied to your broader business goals. Do you want to increase sales, enhance customer loyalty, or boost brand recognition? Each of these goals can be measured through various metrics, such as sales revenue, customer retention rates, or brand sentiment analysis.

When it comes to Omni-Channel Marketing, you'll want to assess the effectiveness of each channel and the interactions between them. Tools like Google Analytics and marketing automation software can help you gain insights into customer behavior. For instance, you can track how often customers visit your website after receiving a promotional email, or how frequently they make an in-store purchase following online research.

The power of Omni-Channel Marketing lies in its ability to provide a holistic view of your customers. By analyzing data from all channels, you can identify trends, patterns, and opportunities. Perhaps you discover that customers who engage with your brand on social media are more likely to visit your physical stores. This knowledge can inform your future marketing strategies.

Additionally, don't forget the importance of gathering feedback directly from your customers. Conduct surveys, host focus groups, and pay attention to their comments on social media. Their insights can be invaluable in fine-tuning your Omni-Channel approach.

Omni-Channel Marketing is not a luxury; it's a necessity in the modern business landscape. It's about providing your customers with a consistent, integrated, and seamless experience, whether they engage with your brand online, in-store, or through other channels. By bridging the gap between your online and offline efforts, you not only make it convenient for customers but also reinforce the idea that your brand is a cohesive entity. The ability to measure the impact of your Omni-Channel strategies is your compass, guiding you to success and continuous improvement. In the end, it's about understanding that your customers don't see channels; they see your brand, and it's your duty to ensure they see it clearly and consistently.

Chapter 5: Utilize Social Proof and Online Reviews

5.1 The Influence of Social Proof

In the bustling marketplace of today, consumers are faced with an overwhelming array of choices. With products and services lining the digital shelves, how do they decide where to spend their hard-earned money? The answer lies in something deeply ingrained in human psychology: social proof.

Understanding the Psychology of Social Proof

Social proof is the phenomenon by which people look to the actions and behaviors of others to determine their own. It's the idea that if others are doing it, it must be the right thing to do. This psychological phenomenon has a profound impact on our choices as consumers.

Think about it: when you're standing in front of two identical coffee shops, one bustling with a line out the door, and the other empty, which one are you more likely to choose? Most of us would opt for the crowded one, assuming that if so many people are there, it must be good. That's social proof in action.

Understanding the psychology behind social proof is the first step in leveraging its power for your business. It taps into our inherent need for reassurance. We crave validation for our choices, and when we see others making similar choices, it eases our decision-making process. It's a fundamental part of human nature, and as a business owner, you can harness it to your advantage.

Types of Social Proof: Expert, Celebrity, User

Social proof comes in various forms, and understanding these forms is key to applying them effectively in your marketing strategies. Let's break down the three primary types of social proof: expert, celebrity, and user.

Expert Social Proof: This type of social proof relies on endorsements from respected authorities or experts in a particular field. When a renowned chef endorses a brand of cookware or a prominent tech guru recommends a specific gadget, it carries weight. Consumers trust the judgment of experts and are more likely to make purchasing decisions based on their recommendations.

Celebrity Social Proof: Celebrity endorsements have been a staple in advertising for decades. When a famous actor, athlete, or public figure attaches their name to a product or service, it automatically gains credibility. The assumption is that if a celebrity believes in it, it must be worth trying.

User Social Proof: User-generated social proof is perhaps the most powerful of all. It's the voice of the everyday consumer who shares their experiences, opinions, and reviews. In the digital age, user social proof has exploded with the advent of online reviews and testimonials. When potential customers read about the positive experiences of others, it strongly influences their purchasing decisions.

Leveraging Social Proof in Marketing

So, how can businesses tap into the power of social proof to boost their marketing efforts? Let's dive into some practical strategies.

Highlight Expert Endorsements: If your product or service has earned the approval of industry experts or professionals, don't keep it a secret. Showcase these endorsements prominently on your website, in your marketing materials, and within product descriptions. When potential customers see that recognized authorities vouch for your offerings, it builds trust.

Embrace Celebrity Influence: While not every business can secure a celebrity endorsement, influencer marketing has become a viable alternative. Partner with micro-influencers in your niche or industry to promote your products or services. Their followers are often highly engaged and trust their recommendations.

Harness User Reviews and Testimonials: The heart of social proof lies in the experiences of your customers. Encourage and collect user-generated content, including reviews, testimonials, and case studies. Feature them prominently on your website and in your marketing campaigns. Positive reviews are like gold in the world of social proof, and they can significantly influence potential customers.

Use Numbers and Statistics: Quantitative social proof is another effective approach. When you can showcase data like "Over 10,000 satisfied customers" or "Rated 4.8 out of

5 stars by our users," it reinforces the idea that your product or service is widely accepted and highly regarded.

Showcase Social Media Engagement: The number of followers, likes, shares, and comments on your social media profiles also acts as a form of social proof. A robust online presence suggests popularity and engagement. It's an indirect way of conveying that people are interested in your brand.

Incorporating social proof into your marketing strategy isn't just a smart move; it's a necessity in today's competitive business landscape. It's a way to connect with your audience on a fundamental level by assuring them that they're making the right choice. By understanding the psychology of social proof and applying it effectively, you can elevate your business and strengthen your customer relationships. In a world of countless options, social proof is the guiding light that leads consumers to your door.

5.2 The Power of Online Reviews

In the digital age, online reviews have become the modern-day word of mouth. The impact of online reviews on buying decisions is nothing short of transformative. They have turned consumers into a powerful force, shaping the fate of businesses and products. In this section, we'll delve into the undeniable influence of online reviews, explore the art of gathering and managing them, and equip you with essential strategies for dealing with the inevitable negative reviews.

The Impact of Online Reviews on Buying Decisions

Online reviews have become the first stop for many consumers on their path to making a purchase. Whether they're looking for a new restaurant to try, a hotel to stay at, or a product to buy, online reviews are their trusted companions in the decision-making process. But why do they carry such weight, and how do they impact buying decisions?

Imagine this scenario: you're planning a vacation to an unfamiliar city, and you want to book a hotel. You open your web browser and type in the name of the city followed by "hotels." Almost instantly, you're presented with a list of options. What's your next move? More often than not, you click on the first hotel that catches your eye. You scroll down, and there they are—those stars, typically on a scale of one to five, glowing next to each hotel's name.

These stars are more than just graphic design elements; they represent the aggregate of countless opinions and experiences from past guests. The more stars, the better the hotel is perceived to be. But it doesn't stop there. You click on the first hotel and start reading the reviews.

Here's where the magic happens. You encounter detailed accounts from people who have stayed at the hotel. They talk about the cleanliness of the rooms, the friendliness of the staff, the quality of the breakfast, and even the view from the window. Some share stories of exceptional experiences, while others might highlight any issues they encountered. As you read through these reviews, a picture of the hotel begins to form in your mind. You start to imagine yourself in the lobby, checking in at the front desk, and enjoying the amenities.

The impact of these reviews on your buying decision is profound. They provide a sense of reassurance or, in some cases, caution. They help you gauge what to expect and allow you to align your expectations with reality. This power to inform and guide consumers is why online reviews matter so much.

For businesses, the significance of this impact is clear. Positive reviews act as virtual recommendations, attracting potential customers and reassuring them that their money will be well spent. Negative reviews, on the other hand, can deter customers and damage the reputation of a business. In both cases, online reviews are instrumental in shaping the perceptions of potential buyers and influencing their choices.

Gathering and Managing Online Reviews
The second crucial aspect of the online review realm is understanding how to gather and manage reviews effectively. Encouraging your satisfied customers to leave reviews can significantly impact your online presence and reputation.

The art of gathering online reviews begins with delivering an exceptional customer experience. Satisfied customers are more likely to take the time to share their positive experiences. Engage with your customers, ask for their feedback, and express your gratitude for their business. This personal touch can motivate them to leave reviews.

To facilitate the review-gathering process, make it easy for customers to write and submit reviews. Provide direct links to review platforms on your website or in post-purchase emails. It's all about reducing friction and making the review process seamless.

Now, let's talk about the critical aspect of managing online reviews. Every review, whether positive or negative, demands a response. Positive reviews deserve appreciation and acknowledgment. Responding with gratitude not only shows your customers that you value their feedback but also encourages others to leave reviews.

Negative reviews, on the other hand, present an opportunity for you to display exceptional customer service. It's not about arguing with the reviewer or dismissing their concerns. It's about addressing the issue, apologizing for any inconvenience, and demonstrating your commitment to resolving the problem. A thoughtful response can often turn a negative review into a positive impression for potential customers.

Strategies for Dealing with Negative Reviews

Negative reviews are an inevitable part of the online landscape. No business is immune to them. However, the way you handle negative reviews can set you apart and even enhance your reputation.

First and foremost, approach negative reviews with a calm and empathetic mindset. Take the time to understand the customer's perspective, and resist the urge to be defensive. Remember that your response is not just for the reviewer but for the entire audience reading the review.

Acknowledge the issue and express your willingness to address it. Offer to take the conversation offline if necessary. This shows that you are genuinely interested in resolving the problem, not just appeasing the customer for the sake of public relations.

Furthermore, use negative reviews as an opportunity for improvement. Consider whether there is a recurring issue mentioned in several reviews. If so, it may be an area that requires attention and action. By learning from negative feedback and making changes, you can turn criticism into growth.

Online reviews have become a potent force in the world of business and commerce. They exert a remarkable influence on consumers' buying decisions, impacting the reputation and success of businesses. Gathering and managing online reviews effectively is an art, one that involves delivering an outstanding customer experience and responding thoughtfully to feedback. When it comes to negative reviews, the key is to handle them with empathy and turn them into opportunities for growth. By mastering the art of online reviews, businesses can harness the power of social proof and build trust with their customers.

5.3 Building Trust and Credibility

In a world where consumers are constantly bombarded with choices, it's imperative for businesses to not only grab their attention but also retain it. Building trust and credibility is the cornerstone of this endeavor. In this section, we will delve into the strategies that can help you gain the confidence of your customers and, in turn, transform them into advocates for your brand.

Showcasing Positive Customer Feedback

The foundation of trust lies in transparency. Your customers need to know that they are making informed decisions, and the best way to facilitate this is by showcasing positive customer feedback. This isn't about cherry-picking the best reviews and testimonials but rather about providing an accurate representation of your product or service.

Start by curating authentic, unfiltered testimonials. These should be in the customers' own words, unvarnished and genuine. Share success stories that highlight how your product or service has made a real difference in your customers' lives. People relate to these stories because they can envision themselves in a similar scenario.

Additionally, be sure to display customer reviews prominently on your website or product pages. When prospective customers can easily find what others are saying about your offering, it builds trust. Consider utilizing review platforms like Yelp, TripAdvisor, or Google Reviews, as well as industry-specific review sites, depending on your business.

Transparency goes a long way in building trust. If a customer has concerns or criticisms, don't hide them. Address them head-on. This shows that you value all customer feedback, not just the positive remarks. By openly acknowledging and responding to negative reviews, you demonstrate a commitment to improvement and accountability.

Encouraging Customers to Leave Reviews
In the era of social proof, it's crucial to encourage your satisfied customers to leave reviews. Their authentic feedback can sway potential buyers in your favor. Here are some strategies to consider:

Firstly, make the process as effortless as possible. Provide clear and easy-to-follow instructions on how to leave a review. This may include links in your email communications, on your website, or through a dedicated review request form.

Timing is essential. Send your review requests at the right moment, ideally after a customer has had a positive experience with your product or service. This could be immediately following a purchase, after a successful interaction with customer support, or after the completion of a service. Fresh in their minds, customers are more likely to share their positive experiences.

Incentives can also be a motivator. Offering a small discount, a gift, or even entry into a giveaway for leaving a review can encourage customers to take that extra step. However, be cautious not to cross ethical lines or compromise the authenticity of the reviews.

Don't underestimate the power of a personal request. If your customer support team has developed a rapport with a customer, they can tactfully ask for a review. A sincere, personal ask often yields more positive results than automated requests.

Harness the influence of social media. Encourage customers to share their experiences and tag your brand. Their social network is more likely to trust recommendations from friends and family.

Responding to Reviews and Demonstrating Accountability

Customers appreciate businesses that are accountable and responsive. When they take the time to leave a review, whether positive or negative, they want to know that they've been heard. Responding to reviews not only acknowledges their efforts but also showcases your commitment to customer satisfaction.

When responding to positive reviews, express your gratitude. Thank the customer for taking the time to share their positive experience. Highlight specific aspects of their feedback, which shows that you genuinely read and appreciated their words.

For negative reviews, it's essential to handle them with care. First and foremost, don't take them personally. It's an opportunity for improvement, not an attack. Address the customer's concerns in a respectful and empathetic manner. Offer a solution or steps to rectify the situation. If the issue is more complex, direct the conversation offline, either through email or a direct message, to avoid public back-and-forths.

Demonstrate accountability by committing to continuous improvement based on the feedback received. Share how you plan to address the issue or prevent it in the future. Customers want to see that their feedback leads to tangible changes.

Remember that your responses are public, and potential customers are watching. A well-managed response to a negative review can actually boost your credibility and trustworthiness. It shows that you care about your customers' experiences and are willing to go the extra mile to make things right.

The power of social proof and online reviews cannot be understated in today's business landscape. Building trust and credibility is not about tricks or gimmicks; it's about transparency, authenticity, and accountability. By showcasing genuine customer feedback, encouraging reviews, and responding effectively, you'll solidify your brand's reputation and turn satisfied customers into advocates who speak volumes for your business. Trust is the currency of the digital age, and it's worth its weight in gold.

Chapter 6: The Secret to Converting Loyal Customers into Your Sales Force

6.1 Turning Customers into Advocates

In the dynamic world of modern business, where competition is fierce and customers are increasingly discerning, there exists a hidden goldmine that can turn the tides in your favor. This concealed gem is the power of transforming loyal customers into your dedicated sales force. In this chapter, we will delve into the art and science of this transformation, unveiling the secret that can fuel your business growth like never before.

Understanding Customer Advocacy

Customer advocacy is more than just a buzzword; it's a strategic approach that can supercharge your business. To grasp its essence, think of your most satisfied customers as your secret weapon. These individuals have experienced your product or service firsthand and emerged not just as satisfied buyers, but as passionate advocates. They're not merely content; they're eager to share their positive experiences with others.

Understanding customer advocacy requires recognizing that your customers become your brand's best ambassadors when they genuinely believe in what you offer. Their advocacy isn't solely fueled by incentives or commissions; it's grounded in trust and authenticity. Advocates trust your brand because it has consistently delivered on its promises, and they feel that their friends and peers will benefit from this trust as well.

Harnessing customer advocacy starts with identifying your advocates. These are the customers who not only use your product or service but also actively recommend it to others, whether through word-of-mouth conversations, online reviews, or social media shout-outs. Advocates aren't just customers; they are partners in your success. They play a vital role in creating a sense of community around your brand.

So, how do you recognize these passionate advocates? Look for customers who regularly engage with your brand, participate in loyalty programs, leave positive reviews, and refer friends and family. Analyze your data, paying close attention to those who consistently interact with your brand in a positive way. Identify your most loyal customers; they are your potential advocates.

Harnessing Word-of-Mouth Marketing

Word-of-mouth marketing, the age-old practice of customers sharing their experiences and recommendations with friends and acquaintances, remains a powerful tool in the digital age. It's an organic, authentic form of marketing that carries substantial weight. Harnessing word-of-mouth marketing means tapping into this naturally occurring phenomenon and directing it toward your advantage.

Advocates are the catalysts for word-of-mouth marketing. They are the enthusiastic individuals who can create a ripple effect within their social circles. Their personal endorsements carry a level of trust and credibility that traditional advertising cannot replicate. Consider a friend recommending a product versus an ad on a billboard; the former usually holds more weight.

To harness word-of-mouth marketing effectively, cultivate your advocates and encourage them to share their experiences. Offer them tools and resources to make advocacy easy and rewarding. This may include providing shareable content, referral programs, or exclusive incentives. Remember, the key to successful word-of-mouth marketing lies in the authenticity of the message. Advocates must genuinely believe in your product and brand to convey their recommendations with sincerity.

Creating a community of advocates who actively engage with your brand and spread the word is a long-term investment. It's not about a quick, one-time sale but about building lasting relationships. These advocates are your extended sales force, working tirelessly to attract new customers and solidify your brand's reputation. Their impact is immeasurable, both in terms of revenue and trust.

Creating Customer Stories and Testimonials
Customer stories and testimonials are the concrete evidence of your advocates' impact. These are the stories of real people who have benefited from your product or service, and they hold immense persuasive power. By creating and sharing customer stories and testimonials, you provide

potential customers with tangible proof of the value your brand offers.

Creating compelling customer stories and testimonials begins by identifying the most impactful customer experiences. Reach out to your advocates and ask them to share their journey with your brand. Encourage them to be authentic and detailed, highlighting the specific ways in which your product or service has positively influenced their lives or businesses.

These stories should resonate with your target audience. They should address pain points, challenges, and desires that your prospective customers can relate to. When a potential customer reads or hears a story from someone who has faced similar struggles and found a solution in your offering, it builds a sense of trust and empathy.

Testimonials are a condensed version of these stories. They are brief, yet potent endorsements that capture the essence of a customer's positive experience. They often include quotes, ratings, or endorsements that are easily digestible for potential customers browsing your website or product listings.

Sharing these stories and testimonials across your marketing channels, whether it's on your website, in email campaigns, or on social media, humanizes your brand. It reinforces the idea that real people have benefited from what you offer. Customer stories and testimonials evoke trust and confidence, prompting potential customers to take action.

The secret to converting loyal customers into your sales force lies in recognizing the advocacy potential within your customer base, nurturing advocates, and leveraging their word-of-mouth marketing and authentic stories. This is not just a marketing strategy; it's a testament to the lasting impact of exceptional customer experiences and the cultivation of loyal advocates who willingly become your brand's most compelling advocates. This is the power that can propel your business to new heights and keep it there for years to come.

6.2 Creating Referral Programs

In the realm of business, it's no secret that loyal customers are a goldmine. These are the individuals who believe in your brand, your products, and the value you provide. They are not only willing to return to your business for repeat purchases but are also likely to spread the word about your offerings. Leveraging these loyal customers to act as your sales force is a strategic move that can elevate your business to new heights.

Designing Effective Referral Programs

When you decide to harness the potential of your loyal customers as advocates for your brand, one of the first steps is to design an effective referral program. This is your blueprint, the roadmap that will guide both your advocates and their referrals toward a mutually beneficial relationship with your business.

An effective referral program has several key components:

Clear Communication: Your program should be crystal clear, leaving no room for ambiguity. Loyal customers need to understand how the program works, what's in it for them, and what's expected of them.

Incentives: Incentives are the heart of your referral program. What's in it for your advocates? Discounts, cash rewards, exclusive access, or other perks? Choose incentives that resonate with your target audience and align with your brand.

Ease of Use: A referral program should be user-friendly. This means that advocates and their referrals should be able to navigate it with ease. A complicated, convoluted program can deter even the most loyal customers from participating.

Tracking and Analytics: To ensure the program's success, it's crucial to track its performance. Implement tracking and analytics tools to monitor referral activity, conversions, and the overall impact on your business.

But why is designing an effective referral program essential? It's because such a program is the bridge between having loyal customers and turning them into your sales force. When it's well-designed, it becomes a natural extension of the advocacy that already exists within your customer base.

Incentives and Rewards for Advocates

In the realm of referral programs, incentives and rewards are the gears that keep the machine running smoothly. To convert your loyal customers into advocates and eventually into your sales force, you need to provide them with compelling reasons to participate.

Incentives can take various forms, but they all serve the same purpose – to motivate and reward your advocates for bringing new customers to your door.

Discounts and Savings: Offering discounts to both the advocate and the referred customer is a time-tested incentive. It's a win-win situation. Advocates get a reduction in their next purchase, and new customers get a sweet deal on their first interaction with your business.

Cash Rewards: Cash is king, and many advocates are more than happy to receive cash rewards. Consider offering a flat cash bonus for each successful referral. This simplicity often appeals to a broad audience.

Exclusive Access: Some customers value exclusivity over monetary rewards. Providing advocates and their referrals with exclusive access to certain products, services, or events can be a compelling incentive.

Points-Based Systems: A points-based system allows advocates to accumulate points for successful referrals. They can then redeem these points for various rewards, making it a flexible and engaging option.

Now, it's important to note that incentives should align with your target audience and your brand. What might work wonders for one business may not necessarily be as effective for another. Therefore, understanding your customers' preferences and desires is a critical aspect of this process.

Incentives aren't just about enticing advocates to participate. They also play a vital role in showing appreciation to your loyal customers. By providing incentives, you're saying, "We value your loyalty, and we want to reward you for believing in us."

Measuring the Success of Referral Initiatives

Measuring the success of your referral program is essential for its continuous improvement and optimization. You need a clear understanding of what's working and what's not. Here's how you can do that effectively:

Set Clear Metrics: Before launching your referral program, establish the key performance indicators (KPIs) you want to track. This might include the number of referrals, the conversion rate, the lifetime value of referred customers, and the overall impact on sales and revenue.

Use Tracking Software: Invest in referral program software that can help you track and measure the performance of your program. This software can provide valuable insights into referral sources, referral paths, and conversion rates.

A/B Testing: Implement A/B testing to experiment with different elements of your referral program. This can help you optimize the program over time. For example, you can test different incentive structures or referral methods to see which ones yield the best results.

Customer Feedback: Solicit feedback from advocates and referred customers to understand their experience with the program. Their insights can provide valuable information for program enhancement.

Regular Evaluation: Regularly evaluate the performance of your referral program. Look for patterns and trends in referral behavior and be ready to make adjustments as needed.

Data-Driven Decision Making: Use the data you collect to inform your decisions. For example, if you notice that referrals from social media platforms tend to convert at a higher rate, you can allocate more resources to that channel.

Return on Investment (ROI): Calculate the ROI of your referral program. This involves assessing the costs associated with running the program and comparing them to the revenue generated from referred customers. A positive ROI indicates a successful program.

By keeping the program simple, personalizing incentives, and tracking performance, you can create a powerful strategy that not only benefits your advocates but also drives substantial growth for your business.

6.3 Building a Community of Advocates

In the vast landscape of business, there exists a coveted force that money can't buy. These are the brand advocates - customers turned passionate supporters who sing your praises, amplify your message, and bring new business through the door. They're not just satisfied; they're thrilled, and they're willing to shout it from the rooftops. In this section, we'll delve into the mechanics of building a thriving community of advocates.

Customer Advocacy Programs

If you've ever wondered how to turn your loyal customers into advocates, the answer often lies in the systematic approach of customer advocacy programs. These programs are like a well-tuned engine, strategically designed to identify, nurture, and empower your brand's biggest fans.

Customer advocacy programs are the structured framework within which your advocates can thrive. They are a beacon that draws in those already enthusiastic about your business, ready to take the next step in their engagement. Such programs typically entail:

Identification: Advocacy programs begin with the identification of your most fervent supporters. These are the customers who consistently sing your praises, who recommend your product or service to friends and family, and who take the time to write glowing reviews. They are the unsung heroes of your brand.

Rewards and Recognition: A key component of advocacy programs is rewarding and recognizing your advocates. This isn't about buying loyalty but rather expressing your gratitude. Rewards may range from exclusive access to events or products, personalized discounts, or even public acknowledgment on your website or social media channels.

Empowerment: Advocacy programs empower your brand's supporters to do more. They provide the tools and resources necessary for advocates to spread the word effectively. Whether it's sharing referral codes, access to advocacy content, or guidance on how to refer friends, these resources make advocacy easy and rewarding.

Involvement: Your advocates become an integral part of your brand's journey. They often participate in feedback sessions, offering insights and ideas for improvement. Involving them in decision-making fosters a sense of ownership and deeper connection.

Engaging Customers in Brand Conversations

Building a community of advocates isn't a one-way street. It's about engaging your customers in brand conversations, fostering a sense of belonging and active participation. Here's how you can do it:

Open Channels of Communication: Communication is the lifeblood of any relationship, and the same goes for your relationship with your customers. Make it easy for them to reach out, ask questions, or provide feedback. Prompt and personalized responses show that you're listening.

Seek Feedback and Act On It: Your advocates are often the best source of candid feedback. Actively seek their opinions and show that you're committed to improvement. When you implement their suggestions, it's not just about problem-solving; it's a demonstration of their importance in your brand's evolution.

Create Opportunities for Engagement: Foster a sense of community by creating spaces where your customers can engage with your brand and with each other. Online forums, social media groups, or even local events (when possible) are excellent ways to facilitate these conversations.

User-Generated Content: Encourage your advocates to generate content related to your brand. This can include reviews, testimonials, photos, and videos. Sharing these contributions not only validates your advocates but also provides authentic and relatable content for your marketing efforts.

Co-Creation: Involve your advocates in the co-creation of products, services, or content. Whether it's a new product feature, a collaborative blog post, or even a charity initiative, co-creation deepens their sense of ownership and connection to your brand.

Measuring the Impact of Customer Advocacy
In the world of business, if you can't measure it, you can't improve it. Customer advocacy is no exception. You need to assess its impact to understand whether your efforts are

paying off and to make data-driven decisions for your advocacy programs.

Key Metrics for Measuring Customer Advocacy:

Net Promoter Score (NPS): NPS measures customer loyalty and the likelihood of advocacy. It's a straightforward question: "On a scale of 0 to 10, how likely are you to recommend our company to a friend or colleague?" Those who rate 9 or 10 are your potential advocates.

Referral Tracking: Monitoring the number of referrals made by your advocates and their conversion rates provides valuable insights. How many new customers did they bring in, and what's the lifetime value of these customers?

Social Media Engagement: Analyze the engagement levels of your advocates on social media. How often do they mention or tag your brand? Are they actively sharing your content and recommendations?

Customer Lifetime Value (CLV): CLV can tell you the long-term value of customers acquired through advocacy. Are these customers more loyal and valuable than those acquired through other channels?

Advocacy ROI: Calculate the return on investment of your advocacy programs. Compare the costs of running these programs to the revenue generated through referrals and increased loyalty.

Case Studies of Successful Customer Advocacy Programs

To illustrate the power of customer advocacy, let's take a look at a few real-world examples:

1. Airbnb's Superhost Program: Airbnb leveraged its most loyal hosts by creating the "Superhost" program. These hosts receive additional benefits, higher visibility in search results, and a badge that signifies their status. As a result, Superhosts tend to outperform regular hosts in bookings, leading to increased revenue for Airbnb.

2. Starbucks Rewards: Starbucks' rewards program goes beyond free coffee. It engages customers by offering personalized suggestions, providing early access to new products, and even curating playlists for in-store music. This not only keeps customers coming back but also motivates them to advocate for the brand.

3. Dropbox's Referral Program: Dropbox's famous referral program gave free storage to users who referred friends. This simple but effective program helped Dropbox grow from 100,000 to over 4 million users in just 15 months.

These case studies demonstrate that when you focus on turning loyal customers into advocates, the results can be substantial. Customer advocacy isn't just about building a fan club; it's about turning that enthusiasm into a tangible force that drives your sales and brand growth.

Building a community of advocates is a strategic endeavor that requires intention, structure, and a genuine commitment to your customers. It's not merely about chasing numbers but about creating a lasting and authentic relationship between your brand and its most dedicated supporters. When you harness the power of advocates, you're not just gaining salespeople; you're creating a movement, and that's a secret worth sharing.

6.4 Addressing Challenges and Concerns

In the world of business, and indeed in life, challenges and concerns are bound to arise. It's no different when it comes to converting loyal customers into your sales force. In this section, we'll delve into some of the common obstacles you might encounter, and, more importantly, how to address and overcome them.

Handling Negative Feedback and Criticism

Negative feedback and criticism can sting. As a business owner or manager, you've invested time and effort into building a strong customer base, and encountering negativity can be disheartening. However, it's crucial to remember that negative feedback is not necessarily a roadblock; it's often an opportunity in disguise.

First, acknowledge the criticism. Whether it's a harsh online review or a disgruntled customer speaking directly to your team, listen, and acknowledge their concerns. Empathy is key in this phase. Demonstrate that you understand their frustration, even if you believe the criticism is unjust.

Next, take the criticism as a chance to improve. Customers who provide feedback, even negative feedback, are often the ones who care the most. Use their comments as a valuable source of information. Analyze the issues raised and see if there are patterns or recurring problems. This kind of feedback is a gift, as it can help you enhance your product or service.

Don't forget to respond publicly, where appropriate. If the feedback is on a public platform, such as social media or review sites, a public response shows your commitment to addressing issues. Offer a solution or a way to make amends, and invite the customer to contact you directly to discuss the matter further. It's a way of showcasing your dedication to customer satisfaction.

Lastly, follow up. After addressing the concern, whether it's by fixing an issue or providing an explanation, reach out to the customer and ask for their feedback on the resolution. This not only demonstrates your commitment to their satisfaction but also provides an opportunity to turn a detractor into an advocate. If the customer feels their concerns were taken seriously and addressed appropriately, they may become one of your most loyal supporters.

Turning Detractors into Advocates

Now, let's tackle the task of turning detractors into advocates. Every business encounters dissatisfied customers at some point, but the way you handle their dissatisfaction can be a game-changer. Consider these steps:

Start by reaching out. Don't wait for detractors to come to you with their grievances. Proactively contact them and ask for their feedback. Make it clear that their opinions matter and that you genuinely want to address their concerns.

Listen actively and empathize. When speaking with detractors, avoid becoming defensive. Instead, actively listen to their complaints and express empathy. Understand their perspective and acknowledge the validity of their feelings. This can go a long way in diffusing tension.

Apologize sincerely. If your business is at fault, offer a sincere apology. Even if you believe the customer's expectations were unrealistic, acknowledge their disappointment and apologize for any inconvenience they experienced.

Offer solutions. Once you've understood the root of the problem, provide solutions or alternatives. Show that you are committed to making things right and improving their experience with your business.

Follow up and exceed expectations. After implementing solutions, follow up to ensure the customer is satisfied. This is the opportunity to exceed their expectations. Offer a gesture of goodwill, such as a discount on their next purchase or a free service. Going the extra mile can transform a detractor into a vocal advocate.

Encourage them to share their positive experience. If a detractor becomes satisfied with your resolution, don't hesitate to ask if they'd be willing to share their positive experience. Satisfied customers who once had reservations can be powerful advocates. Their authentic stories of transformation can influence others to give your business a chance.

Balancing Customer Advocacy with Brand Authenticity

Balancing customer advocacy with brand authenticity is a delicate dance. While you want to encourage loyal customers to promote your business, it's equally vital to maintain the authenticity and integrity of your brand. Here's how to strike that balance:

Start by setting clear guidelines. Develop guidelines for customer advocates that outline what's acceptable when promoting your business. Emphasize the importance of honesty and authenticity. Ensure your advocates understand that while they can share their positive experiences, they should refrain from making false or misleading claims.

Educate your advocates. Provide your advocates with the information and tools they need to effectively represent your brand. Educate them about your products or services and any key messages you want them to convey. The more informed they are, the more authentic their advocacy will be.

Encourage genuine storytelling. Authenticity is rooted in genuine storytelling. Encourage your advocates to share their real experiences with your business. Authentic stories resonate with other potential customers and build trust.

Monitor and moderate. Keep an eye on how your advocates are representing your brand. Monitor their content and intervene if you notice any inconsistencies or misleading information. This proactive approach ensures that your brand maintains its authenticity.

Reward and recognize. Show your appreciation to your advocates. Recognize their efforts and reward them for their loyalty. This can be done through special discounts, exclusive access, or other incentives. Recognizing their advocacy reinforces their commitment to your brand.

Addressing challenges and concerns, turning detractors into advocates, and balancing customer advocacy with brand authenticity are all essential aspects of converting loyal customers into your sales force. These steps require diligence, empathy, and a commitment to maintaining the authenticity of your brand. When executed effectively, they can turn satisfied customers into enthusiastic advocates, propelling your business to new heights of success.

Chapter 6: The Secret to Converting Loyal Customers into Your Sales Force

6.5 Case Studies from Real World

In the relentless world of business, where every customer interaction counts, there exists an invaluable, yet often untapped, resource that can supercharge your growth: your loyal customers. These are the patrons who not only appreciate your products or services but also serve as willing advocates, propelling your brand into the hearts and minds of others. They are your unpaid sales force, and in this section, we will explore real-world examples of businesses that have harnessed the transformative power of converting loyal customers into dedicated sales ambassadors.

Real-World Examples of Customer-to-Sales Conversion

1. Apple - The Apple Enthusiast Community: Apple, the tech giant renowned for its unwavering customer loyalty, capitalizes on its devoted customer base through its Apple Enthusiast Community. This network of Apple enthusiasts, empowered by their deep love for the brand, actively participates in discussions, provides tech support, and recommends products to friends and family. By nurturing this community, Apple has successfully turned its loyal customers into influential sales advocates.

2. Tesla - The Tesla Owner Network: Tesla, a pioneer in electric vehicles, has cultivated an avid and engaged community of Tesla owners. These owners often become brand evangelists, sharing their experiences and advocating for Tesla's sustainability mission. This organic network has

significantly contributed to Tesla's growth, demonstrating the powerful ripple effect of turning customers into sales ambassadors.

3. Airbnb - Hosts as Promoters: Airbnb, a disruptor in the hospitality industry, has transformed its hosts into dedicated promoters. These hosts, who were once customers themselves, actively recommend Airbnb to potential guests and other potential hosts. By providing them with the tools and incentives to become advocates, Airbnb has harnessed the authentic voices of those who make their platform successful.

Strategies Used by Brands to Leverage Advocates

Turning loyal customers into sales advocates doesn't happen by chance. It requires a well-thought-out strategy that resonates with your customers and encourages them to share their positive experiences. Let's delve into some of the effective strategies that brands have employed to leverage their advocates.

1. Recognition and Rewards: Brands like Amazon have harnessed the power of their customers' voices through programs like "Amazon Vine." This initiative identifies and rewards top reviewers with early access to new products. Recognizing and rewarding customer advocates not only fosters a sense of appreciation but also motivates them to continue promoting your products or services.

2. User-Generated Content: GoPro, the action camera company, thrives on user-generated content. By

encouraging customers to share their exhilarating videos and photos captured with their GoPro cameras, the company has created a vast library of authentic, action-packed content that not only promotes their products but also inspires potential customers.

3. Referral Programs: Dropbox, a cloud storage company, has leveraged its customers' loyalty by introducing a referral program. By offering additional storage space to customers who refer friends and family, Dropbox has harnessed the power of word-of-mouth marketing. This strategy provides a win-win scenario, as loyal customers get more value while the brand acquires new customers.

Lessons Learned from Converting Loyal Customers into Sales Ambassadors

The success stories of businesses that have transformed their loyal customers into sales ambassadors offer invaluable lessons. Here are some key takeaways:

1. Authenticity Matters: Customers who become advocates do so because of their genuine love for your brand. Authenticity is the bedrock of advocacy. Therefore, fostering a culture of authenticity and transparency is essential to attract and retain sales ambassadors.

2. Incentivize Advocacy: Recognizing and rewarding your advocates is a powerful motivator. Whether through referral programs, exclusive access, or simply acknowledging their contributions, incentives can amplify advocacy efforts.

3. Provide the Tools: Brands that excel in leveraging advocates often provide their customers with the tools and resources they need to be effective promoters. Whether it's simple shareable content, referral links, or access to exclusive forums, make it easy for advocates to spread the word.

4. Listen and Adapt: The voice of your customer is a valuable asset. Pay attention to their feedback, both positive and negative. Learn from their experiences and adapt your products, services, and marketing strategies accordingly.

In the realm of business, customer loyalty is the ultimate accolade, and converting loyal customers into your sales force is the crown jewel of your customer relationship strategy. The success stories of brands like Apple, Tesla, and Airbnb demonstrate the profound impact that customer advocates can have on your bottom line. By recognizing their contributions, employing smart strategies, and staying true to the principles of authenticity, your loyal customers can become your most potent sales ambassadors. In doing so, they become more than just patrons; they become passionate partners in your way to success.

Chapter 7: Going Beyond Customer Expectations

7.1 Delivering Exceptional Customer Service

In the relentless pursuit of business success, one thing remains unwavering – the importance of delivering exceptional customer service. It's not just a box to check; it's the bedrock of long-term success. In this section, we delve into the core of this concept, exploring the key aspects of delivering exceptional customer service that sets your business apart.

Setting High Service Standards

Exceptional customer service starts with a commitment to setting high service standards. It's not about occasional bursts of excellence but a consistent dedication to meeting and surpassing customer expectations. These standards are your compass, guiding every interaction your team has with customers. When you set these standards high, you create a culture of excellence that radiates throughout your organization.

So, how do you define these standards? It begins with a thorough understanding of your customer base. You need to grasp their needs, preferences, and pain points. What drives satisfaction for one might not work for another. Create a service framework that takes these nuances into account.

Training is your secret weapon here. Your employees are the front-line soldiers in your service standards campaign.

Equip them with the skills and knowledge to not only meet but exceed those standards. Customer service training is an ongoing process, not a one-time event. It involves continuous learning, coaching, and the empowerment of your team to take initiative in service situations.

But standards don't end with customer interactions. They also extend to consistency and reliability. Are your products or services consistently meeting quality standards? Are your delivery times reliable? Inconsistency erodes trust, and trust is the cornerstone of exceptional service.

Your standards also need to encompass a commitment to transparency. When you make a mistake – because it happens to the best of us – own up to it. Admitting errors and working tirelessly to rectify them can sometimes do more for customer loyalty than never making a mistake at all.

Dealing with Challenging Situations
No matter how high your service standards, challenges will arise. It's during these trying moments that exceptional customer service truly shines. These challenges may come in various forms - from customer complaints to shipping delays. How you handle these situations can define your brand more than any advertising campaign.

The first rule of dealing with challenges is to never shy away from them. Ignoring or avoiding problems only exacerbates the issue. Instead, confront them head-on. Listen actively to customer concerns. Show empathy and understanding. Customers want to know you care about their problems. Even if you can't always offer the immediate solution they desire, showing you value their concerns can go a long way.

When resolving issues, keep in mind that speed matters. Customers don't want to wait around for a response or solution. The quicker you address their concerns, the more likely they are to perceive your service as exceptional. In today's fast-paced world, a timely resolution is a powerful competitive advantage.

Empower your customer service team to make decisions. Provide them with the authority to resolve issues within reasonable limits. This doesn't mean giving away the store, but it means giving your team the ability to make quick decisions to satisfy customers without the need for managerial approvals. This leads to faster problem-solving and more satisfied customers.

Dealing with challenging situations also means learning from them. Every issue is an opportunity for growth. Conduct post-mortems on challenging situations to identify root causes and prevent them from recurring. This not only ensures smoother operations but also demonstrates your commitment to continuous improvement.

The Impact of Outstanding Service
Exceptional customer service isn't just a "nice-to-have" in today's competitive landscape. It's a strategic imperative

that has a profound impact on your business. Let's delve into the tangible benefits of delivering outstanding service:

1. Customer Loyalty: Exceptional service is the key to building long-term customer loyalty. When customers know they can rely on your brand for exceptional service, they're more likely to remain loyal and become repeat buyers. They become your advocates, referring others to your business.

2. Positive Word of Mouth: Exceptional service generates positive word of mouth, which is a potent marketing tool. Satisfied customers are more likely to share their experiences with friends and family, and these endorsements carry weight in the decision-making process of potential customers.

3. Reduced Customer Churn: High service standards keep customers from churning to competitors. When they know they can count on you to meet their needs and resolve issues swiftly, they have little reason to look elsewhere.

4. Increased Profits: Satisfied and loyal customers tend to spend more with your business. They are willing to pay a premium for the quality and service they receive. Exceptional service, therefore, translates into increased profits.

5. Improved Employee Morale: Happy and engaged employees are more likely to deliver exceptional service. When employees see the positive impact of their efforts on customer satisfaction and the company's success, their morale improves.

6. Competitive Advantage: Exceptional service sets you apart from the competition. In a world where products and services are often similar, it's the level of service that becomes the distinguishing factor.

Delivering exceptional customer service is not just a noble pursuit; it's a strategic move with profound implications for your business. Setting high service standards, addressing challenging situations, and understanding the real impact of outstanding service will help you establish a culture of excellence that, in turn, attracts and retains loyal customers who become your most powerful sales force. Exceptional service isn't a luxury; it's a necessity in the modern business landscape.

7.2 Creating Delightful Surprises

In the world of business, meeting customer expectations is merely the baseline. It's a good start, but it's not enough. To truly win the hearts and loyalty of your customers, you need to go the extra mile. You need to surprise and delight them in ways they never saw coming. And this, my friends, is where the magic happens.

Moments of Wow: Unexpected Acts of Kindness

Picture this: you walk into your favorite coffee shop, and the barista, who knows you by name, hands you your usual morning pick-me-up. But this time, there's a warm, freshly baked chocolate chip cookie resting on the saucer. That's a moment of wow. It's a simple act of kindness that takes an ordinary transaction and turns it into something extraordinary.

The power of these moments of wow lies in their unexpectedness. They catch your customers off guard, leaving them pleasantly surprised and with a smile on their face. It could be a complimentary dessert at a restaurant, a handwritten thank-you note in a package, or a free upgrade on a flight. These moments have the potential to leave a lasting impression.

Look the Ritz-Carlton, for example. They're known for their legendary customer service. If a guest at one of their hotels forgets a personal item, say a laptop charger, the Ritz-Carlton team doesn't just return the forgotten item. They return it with a bow, a smile, and a sense of urgency. It's not just meeting expectations; it's exceeding them in a way that creates a moment of wow.

But creating moments of wow isn't just about material gestures. It's about emotional connections. Think about the last time someone did something unexpected and kind for you. It wasn't just the action itself; it was the fact that they thought of you. They considered your needs, your comfort, and your happiness. And that's the essence of creating wow moments in your business.

To implement this in your business, you need to empower your team to think creatively and act spontaneously. Encourage them to pay attention to the little details, to pick up on cues from your customers, and to seize the opportunity to make someone's day a bit brighter. Moments of wow don't have to be grand; they just have to be heartfelt.

Personalized Gifts and Gestures

In the digital age, personalization has become a buzzword in the business world. But it's not just a buzzword; it's a critical component of creating delightful surprises. When you take the time to know your customers, to understand their preferences and history with your business, you can tailor your gestures in a way that's truly meaningful to them.

Let's take the example of a high-end boutique. A loyal customer receives a beautifully wrapped package in the mail. Inside, she finds not just the dress she ordered, but also a handpicked accessory that perfectly complements her style. It's not a random gift; it's a personalized gesture that shows the boutique cares about her as an individual.

This level of personalization requires data and insight into your customers. It's not about generic mass emails with the customer's name plugged in; it's about understanding their past purchases, their browsing history, and their preferences. It's about anticipating their needs before they even realize them.

Moreover, personalization extends beyond product recommendations. It's about creating a sense of belonging. When a customer feels like you understand them on a personal level, they're more likely to remain loyal to your brand. They become more than just a transaction; they become a part of your community.

Creating personalized gifts and gestures isn't solely about increasing sales. It's about building relationships. When your customers know you're paying attention to them, they're more likely to stick around. They become your brand advocates, singing your praises to friends and family.

The Role of Personal Touch in Customer Delight

At the core of creating delightful surprises is the personal touch. It's about making your customers feel valued, appreciated, and seen as individuals rather than numbers. The personal touch can manifest in numerous ways, from handwritten notes to remembering customers' preferences to the tone of your communication.

Think about a small local bookstore. The owner knows most of their customers by name. When you walk in, they ask about the book you purchased last time and recommend something you might enjoy based on your reading history. That personal touch creates an intimate connection that keeps customers coming back.

The personal touch doesn't have to be complicated or expensive. It's about the effort you put into making your customers feel special. It's about making them feel like they matter, and their business is genuinely appreciated.

Remember that the personal touch is not just the responsibility of your customer service team; it should permeate your entire organization. It's the friendly greeting from your receptionist, the helpfulness of your sales team, and the genuine interest of your support staff. It's the embodiment of your brand's commitment to going beyond customer expectations.

Incorporating the personal touch into your business culture involves training your employees to be genuinely caring and attentive. It's about fostering a company culture that prioritizes empathy and connection with customers. It's not something you can fake; it has to come from a place of sincerity.

Going beyond customer expectations is not just a business strategy; it's a philosophy. It's a commitment to creating experiences that are not only memorable but also deeply personal. Moments of wow, personalized gifts and gestures, and the personal touch are the tools at your disposal to make that philosophy a reality in your business. When you surprise and delight your customers in these ways, you're not just building a customer base; you're creating a loyal, dedicated community of brand advocates. And that, my friends, is where the real magic of customer magnetism happens.

7.3 Building Long-Term Customer Trust

In today's fast-paced business environment, where customers have a multitude of choices at their fingertips, building long-term trust is more critical than ever. Consistency, transparency, and honesty are the cornerstones of establishing this trust, and in this section, we'll delve into these key elements, providing real-world examples of brands that have mastered the art of exceeding customer expectations.

Consistency in Quality and Service

Consistency, both in the quality of your products or services and in your approach to customer service, is the foundation upon which long-term trust is built. Customers need to know that they can rely on your brand to deliver the same level of excellence every time they interact with you.

When we talk about consistency in quality, we're not just referring to meeting customer expectations; it's about consistently exceeding them. This means setting high standards for your products or services and holding yourself accountable to meet and surpass those standards consistently.

Let's take Apple Inc. as a prime example. For years, Apple has been known for producing high-quality, user-friendly products. Their consistency in delivering sleek and innovative devices, from the iPod to the iPhone and MacBook, has fostered unwavering trust among their customer base. When you buy an Apple product, you expect it to work seamlessly, and time after time, Apple delivers on that expectation.

Consistency in customer service is equally vital. It's about ensuring that every customer interaction, whether in-store, online, or through customer support, follows the same principles of respect, helpfulness, and a genuine commitment to resolving customer issues. Consider Amazon, which has set the bar high in terms of customer service consistency. Their dedication to prompt shipping, easy returns, and responsive customer support has made them a prime example of consistency in the e-commerce industry.

The Value of Transparency and Honesty

Transparency and honesty are like the glue that binds a customer and a brand together. It's about revealing the inner workings of your business, acknowledging both your successes and your failures, and always being truthful with your customers. When you're upfront and honest, you gain the respect and trust of your customers.

Take a look at Zappos, an online shoe and clothing retailer. Zappos is known for its radical transparency and honesty. They openly share their company culture, including the concept of "delivering WOW through service." They don't just sell shoes; they sell a culture of exceptional customer service. Zappos even encourages customers to call their customer service team for any reason, not just to make a purchase. This level of transparency and honesty has built a loyal following of customers who trust Zappos as a brand that genuinely cares about their satisfaction.

Another aspect of transparency and honesty is admitting when you've made a mistake. Customers understand that no business is perfect, but they appreciate it when a brand takes responsibility for errors and takes steps to correct them. The simple act of saying, "We made a mistake, and here's how we're going to fix it," can turn a potentially negative experience into a positive one. This level of honesty and transparency shows customers that you value their trust more than a short-term gain.

Case Studies of Brands that Exceed Expectations

To truly understand the significance of building long-term customer trust by consistently exceeding expectations, let's dive into a few compelling case studies of brands that have mastered this art:

Ritz-Carlton: The Ritz-Carlton Hotel Company is renowned for its impeccable service. Every employee is empowered to go to great lengths to meet guests' needs. From remembering guest preferences to addressing special requests, they consistently deliver top-notch service, leaving guests not just satisfied but wowed. This level of service has resulted in a loyal customer base that keeps returning for the exceptional experience.

Tesla: Tesla, the electric vehicle manufacturer, is known for consistently exceeding expectations in product innovation. With each new model, they push the boundaries of electric vehicle technology, offering not just a car but an experience. Tesla's transparency regarding their product's capabilities, continuous software updates, and emphasis on sustainability have gained the trust of eco-conscious consumers and tech enthusiasts alike.

Southwest Airlines: Southwest Airlines has built a loyal following through consistent service excellence. They are renowned for their friendly and helpful staff, affordable pricing, and a customer-centric approach. Customers trust Southwest because they consistently receive great value and a positive flying experience, making them one of the most preferred airlines in the United States.

Going beyond customer expectations is not merely a one-time feat but a consistent practice that requires dedication, transparency, and honesty. When you consistently exceed customer expectations in both product/service quality and customer service, you build long-term trust that fosters loyalty and advocacy. These brands have shown us that it's not a matter of merely meeting customer expectations, but exceeding them consistently that transforms customers into devoted advocates.

Chapter 8: Foster a Customer-Centric Culture

8.1 The Role of Leadership

A customer-centric culture doesn't just happen; it's cultivated, nurtured, and driven from the top down. In this section, we delve into the pivotal role of leadership in fostering a customer-centric culture. We'll explore how a customer-centric CEO can lead by example, align leadership with customer priorities, and effectively communicate the vision throughout the organization.

Leadership within an organization is the rudder that guides the ship. If leaders don't prioritize the customer experience and lead by example, it's unlikely that the organization as a whole will develop a truly customer-centric mindset.

Leading by Example: A Customer-Centric CEO

At the helm of any organization, the CEO's influence is unparalleled. A customer-centric CEO doesn't just talk the talk; they walk the walk. They lead by example, setting the standard for customer-centricity that others throughout the organization will follow.

A customer-centric CEO recognizes that every decision they make, from strategic choices to daily interactions, should be evaluated through the lens of how it will impact the customer. This means going beyond profit margins and considering how each action aligns with the values and needs of the customer base.

Take, for example, a scenario where a product is ready for launch, but quality issues have arisen. A customer-centric CEO will delay the launch if it's in the best interest of the customers, even if it means short-term financial setbacks. Their unwavering commitment to putting the customer's needs first sends a powerful message to the entire organization that customer satisfaction is paramount.

Aligning Leadership with Customer Priorities

The CEO can't champion a customer-centric culture alone; they need a leadership team that shares the vision. To foster such alignment, leaders at all levels must be educated about the organization's customer-centric goals and the role they play in achieving them.

Leaders should be encouraged to internalize the customer's perspective. This goes beyond understanding market research; it involves experiencing the customer journey themselves. It's about leaders getting their hands dirty, working the frontlines, and truly grasping the challenges and aspirations of the customers their organization serves.

An aligned leadership team will naturally prioritize customer-centric initiatives, and this alignment often trickles down through the organization, as leaders communicate, embody, and reinforce these priorities.

Communicating the Vision Throughout the Organization

To build and sustain a customer-centric culture, it's crucial that the vision is communicated effectively throughout the entire organization. This involves clear, consistent, and engaging messaging that resonates with employees at all levels.

One of the most effective ways to instill the customer-centric vision is through storytelling. Stories humanize the concept, making it relatable and emotionally engaging. Sharing stories of customer success, stories of how employees made a difference in a customer's life, and stories that highlight the positive impact of a customer-centric approach serve as powerful motivators.

Another critical aspect of communicating the vision is transparency. Employees need to understand the "why" behind the customer-centric approach. This transparency enables them to see the bigger picture and appreciate the importance of their role in the larger narrative.

Regular communication channels, such as company-wide meetings, newsletters, and even social platforms within the organization, can serve as vehicles for reinforcing the customer-centric vision. Leadership should consistently emphasize that everyone within the organization has a role in fulfilling the vision, whether they're on the frontlines or in the back office.

Fostering a customer-centric culture is not an abstract aspiration but a concrete, attainable goal. Leadership, particularly the CEO, plays a pivotal role in making this vision a reality. Leading by example, aligning leadership with customer priorities, and effectively communicating the vision throughout the organization are the building blocks of a truly customer-centric culture. It's not just about saying you're customer-centric; it's about living it every day and embedding it into the DNA of your organization. In the end, it's a commitment that pays off in the form of customer loyalty, sustainable growth, and a resilient competitive edge in the market.

8.2 Employee Training and Empowerment

One key to success to foster a customer-centric culture lies in the skill and empowerment of your employees. The very individuals who interact with your customers day in and day out are the linchpins that hold your customer-centric approach together. In this section, we delve deep into the heart of your workforce, exploring how to equip them with the necessary skills, encourage their initiative, and empower frontline staff to create meaningful customer interactions.

Equipping Employees with Customer-Centric Skills

In today's competitive business landscape, simply having a product or service is not enough to stand out. What truly sets a business apart is the way its employees engage with customers. This is where the importance of equipping employees with customer-centric skills becomes evident.

Imagine a scenario where your employees can seamlessly put themselves in the shoes of your customers. They understand their needs, anticipate their questions, and proactively offer solutions. This level of customer empathy is the bedrock of a customer-centric culture.

To achieve this, structured training is crucial. This isn't about a one-time orientation; it's an ongoing process that empowers employees to grow continuously. The training should cover:

A. Understanding Customer Needs: Equip your employees with the ability to listen actively to customers, extract their pain points, and genuinely understand their requirements. This means not just hearing words but decoding the underlying needs.

B. Effective Communication: Communication isn't just about what you say, but how you say it. Train your employees to communicate clearly, empathetically, and in a manner that resonates with customers.

C. Problem Solving: Equip your team with problem-solving skills. They should be adept at thinking on their feet, offering solutions, and, when needed, seeking help efficiently. A resourceful employee is a valuable asset.

D. Product Knowledge: Your employees should be product or service experts. They should know the ins and outs, benefits, and potential pitfalls. This knowledge is crucial in guiding customers effectively.

E. Handling Difficult Situations: Not every customer interaction is a smooth sail. Empower your employees to handle difficult situations with grace and confidence. This is where a calm demeanor, empathy, and active listening skills shine.

Encouraging Employee Initiative

Empowering employees to take initiative is a fundamental building block of a customer-centric culture. It goes beyond merely doing what's expected; it's about employees proactively identifying opportunities to improve the customer experience. When employees take the initiative, they become proactive problem solvers and valuable brand ambassadors.

Encouraging employee initiative can be achieved through several strategies:

A. Open Communication Channels: Employees should feel comfortable sharing their ideas and concerns. They should know that their feedback is valued and that it can lead to meaningful changes in the organization.

B. Autonomy: Give employees the freedom to make decisions within their areas of responsibility. When they have ownership over their work, they're more likely to take the initiative to make improvements.

C. Recognition and Reward: Acknowledge and reward employees for taking the initiative. This can be in the form of incentives, recognition programs, or career advancement opportunities. When employees see that their efforts are appreciated, they're motivated to do more.

D. Continuous Learning: Provide opportunities for employees to develop new skills and knowledge. This not only equips them to take the initiative but also fosters a culture of continuous improvement.

E. Lead by Example: Leadership plays a crucial role in encouraging initiative. When leaders lead by example and demonstrate a willingness to take risks and make improvements, it sets the tone for the entire organization.

Remember, employee initiative doesn't just benefit customers but the organization as a whole. It leads to innovation, process improvements, and a positive work environment.

Empowering Frontline Staff for Better Customer Interactions
Frontline staff are the face of your business. They are the first point of contact for customers and bear the responsibility of leaving a lasting impression. Empowering them for better customer interactions is pivotal in building a customer-centric culture.

Here's how you can empower your frontline staff effectively:

A. Clear Guidelines: Provide clear guidelines and policies that empower frontline staff to make decisions in the best interest of the customer. When employees know what's expected and have the flexibility to act accordingly, they can respond to customer needs more effectively.

B. Training and Skill Development: Invest in ongoing training and skill development for your frontline staff. This includes not only customer service skills but also problem-solving, conflict resolution, and effective communication.

C. Access to Information: Ensure that your frontline staff has quick access to the information they need to serve customers. Whether it's product information, customer history, or support resources, easy access is key to quick, accurate responses.

D. Empathy and Active Listening: Encourage and cultivate empathy in your frontline staff. Empathy is the foundation of understanding and meeting customer needs. Active listening skills are equally important to ensure customers feel heard and valued.

E. Support and Recognition: Provide a support system for frontline staff. Recognize their efforts and be available to address their concerns. When employees feel supported, they're more confident and capable in their roles.

Employee training and empowerment are not merely components of a customer-centric culture; they are the engines that drive it forward. When your employees are equipped with customer-centric skills, encouraged to take initiative, and empowered for better customer interactions, they become the driving force that converts satisfied customers into lifelong advocates and brand ambassadors. It's not just about what you sell; it's about how you serve your customers, and your employees are the key to unlocking that potential.

8.3 Measuring and Rewarding Customer-Centricity

In our journey to creating a truly customer-centric culture within your organization, we've covered the vital aspects of leadership commitment and employee training. Now, as we delve into the final section, it's time to understand how to measure and reward the manifestation of customer-centricity within your company.

Key Performance Indicators for a Customer-Centric Culture

The success of any cultural shift within an organization depends on its ability to be quantified and evaluated. This is where Key Performance Indicators (KPIs) come into play. KPIs are a set of specific, measurable metrics that gauge the progress of your customer-centric transformation.

One of the most fundamental KPIs is customer satisfaction. Customer surveys, feedback forms, and Net Promoter Scores (NPS) can help you assess how satisfied your customers are with your products or services. Tracking changes in customer satisfaction over time gives you a clear picture of the impact of your customer-centric efforts.

Additionally, customer retention rate is a crucial KPI. It reveals how effectively you're keeping your existing customers and preventing churn. A higher retention rate often indicates that your customer-centric strategies are working.

Let's not forget the Customer Lifetime Value (CLV) as a KPI. It tells you how much a customer is worth to your business over the course of their relationship with you. An increasing CLV suggests that your efforts to build lasting customer relationships are paying off.

Lastly, response and resolution times in customer service are valuable KPIs. The faster you respond to customer inquiries and resolve their issues, the more you exhibit a customer-centric approach. Reduced response times often lead to improved customer experiences.

Recognizing and Rewarding Customer-Centric Actions

Now that you have a set of KPIs to measure your progress, it's time to consider how to recognize and reward those within your organization who embody the customer-centric culture you aim to cultivate.

Recognition doesn't always have to come in the form of monetary incentives. While financial rewards can be effective, non-monetary recognition can be equally powerful. Acknowledgment during team meetings, a simple "thank you" note, or public praise can go a long way in motivating employees to continue prioritizing customer-centric actions.

Setting up a recognition program that spotlights individuals or teams who consistently display customer-centric behaviors fosters a culture of appreciation and encourages others to follow suit. These programs might include

"Customer Champion of the Month" awards or "Customer-Centric Team of the Quarter" honors.

It's important to tailor your recognition and rewards to your organizational culture. Consider what resonates most with your employees. Some may prefer financial bonuses, while others may value personal growth opportunities or additional time off. Recognize that what motivates one team member may differ from what motivates another.

Fostering a Culture of Continuous Improvement
A truly customer-centric culture is not static but continuously evolving. It requires a commitment to perpetual growth and learning. A culture of continuous improvement revolves around the idea that there is always a better way to do things, and your employees are encouraged to actively seek out those improvements.

Start by creating open channels for feedback. Encourage employees at all levels to share their insights and suggestions. This can be facilitated through regular surveys, suggestion boxes, or open forums. Acknowledge the value of their input, even if every suggestion can't be implemented.

Establish a structured process for reviewing and implementing improvements. This process should involve cross-functional teams that collaborate to solve problems and make enhancements. It's essential to have mechanisms in place to track the progress of these initiatives and communicate the results to the entire organization.

Moreover, foster a culture of experimentation. Encourage employees to try new approaches and techniques in the pursuit of better customer service. It's not about always getting it right on the first try but rather about a willingness to innovate and learn from both successes and failures.

Fostering a customer-centric culture is not just about leadership and training; it's about measuring, recognizing, and continually improving the customer-centric behaviors and processes within your organization. By defining your KPIs, recognizing and rewarding customer-centric actions, and fostering a culture of continuous improvement, you pave the way for enduring success in your quest to put the customer at the center of everything you do.

A customer-centric culture is not a one-off initiative but a commitment to making customer satisfaction a way of life for your organization. It's about creating a workplace where every team member, from the CEO to the frontline staff, understands the vital role they play in delighting customers and, in turn, driving the growth and success of your business.

Chapter 9: Crisis Management and Customer Recovery

9.1 Handling Customer Complaints Effectively

In the relentless world of business, complaints are like hidden treasures waiting to be uncovered. They're not signs of failure; they're opportunities for growth, improvement, and, believe it or not, customer loyalty. The key to handling customer complaints effectively is to embrace them with open arms, rather than dreading them. Let's dive into the crucial art of managing customer grievances with precision and empathy.

The Importance of Listening and Empathy

When a customer reaches out with a complaint, it's a plea for attention, a chance to be heard, and, most importantly, an opportunity for your business to demonstrate empathy. Listening is the cornerstone of effective complaint resolution. It's not just about hearing words; it's about understanding emotions, concerns, and the underlying message.

Imagine this scenario: A customer calls your support line, frustrated and upset because they received a damaged product. They have every right to be unhappy, but how you respond will make all the difference.

Empathy, in this context, means putting yourself in the customer's shoes, feeling their frustration, and acknowledging their disappointment. You might say something like, "I'm really sorry to hear that your product arrived damaged. I can imagine how frustrating that must be." This simple act of acknowledging their feelings can have a profound impact. It makes the customer feel heard and understood, setting the stage for a more positive interaction.

Moreover, effective listening doesn't involve interrupting or rushing to provide a solution. It means allowing the customer to express their concerns fully, asking clarifying questions, and showing that you genuinely care about resolving the issue. Remember, it's not just about solving the problem; it's about making the customer feel valued.

Resolving Issues with Speed and Precision
Listening and empathy set the stage, but it's resolving the issue with speed and precision that truly makes the difference. Once you understand the problem, it's time to take swift and effective action. Customers don't want excuses; they want solutions.

Let's return to our scenario. The customer's product arrived damaged, and you've empathized with their frustration. Now, it's time to resolve the issue. This is where speed and precision come into play. You need to act quickly to rectify the situation.

In this case, you might offer to send a replacement product immediately, free of charge. If that's not possible, you might provide a full refund and offer a discount on their next purchase as a goodwill gesture. The key is to make the customer whole again, to provide a solution that goes above and beyond their expectations.

When you resolve a customer complaint with speed and precision, you demonstrate your commitment to their satisfaction. You turn a negative experience into a positive one, and, in doing so, you can often transform an unhappy customer into a loyal advocate.

It's not just about fixing the issue. It's about doing so with precision, ensuring that the customer doesn't encounter similar problems in the future. You need to address the root cause of the complaint, whether it's a product quality issue, a process flaw, or a communication breakdown.

Turning Negative Experiences into Positives
Now, here's the real secret of effective complaint management: turning negative experiences into positives. It's not merely about resolving the issue at hand; it's about leaving the customer feeling more satisfied than if the issue had never occurred.

Let's revisit our damaged product scenario one more time. You've listened with empathy, resolved the issue with speed and precision, and the customer has a new, undamaged product in their hands. But why stop there? This is your opportunity to go the extra mile.

Consider a handwritten note accompanying the replacement product, expressing your sincere apologies for the inconvenience they experienced. Perhaps you offer a discount on their next purchase, or you provide them with exclusive access to a customer loyalty program. These gestures not only rectify the immediate problem but also create a lasting positive impression.

When customers experience a problem and see your company going above and beyond to make it right, they often become more loyal than if the issue had never happened. It's an opportunity to create what we call the "wow factor," where customers are pleasantly surprised by your commitment to their satisfaction.

In a world where customer service can often be transactional and impersonal, these personal touches set you apart. They show that you care deeply about your customers, their experiences, and their loyalty.

The art of effective complaint management is a powerful tool in building customer loyalty. By listening with empathy, resolving issues with speed and precision, and turning negative experiences into positives, you can not only retain customers but also convert them into enthusiastic advocates for your brand. Every complaint is a chance to demonstrate your commitment to your customers and, in doing so, transform challenges into opportunities for growth and long-lasting relationships.

9.2 Strategies for Recovering Customer Trust
In the world of business, where human interactions are at the core of everything, missteps and errors are inevitable. The true measure of a company's character, though, is how

it responds to these missteps. Crisis management is not merely about firefighting and damage control; it's about acknowledging when things go awry and taking proactive steps to make things right.

Apology: A Humble Act of Accountability

One of the most powerful tools in crisis management is the simple act of apologizing. When something goes wrong, whether it's a product defect, a service lapse, or a misunderstanding, customers are left disappointed, frustrated, and sometimes angry. An apology is the first step in rebuilding the broken trust.

An effective apology goes beyond the generic "We're sorry for any inconvenience this may have caused." It's personal, specific, and empathetic. It acknowledges the issue and the impact it had on the customer. A heartfelt apology conveys not just regret but a deep understanding of the customer's feelings. It says, "We understand what you're going through, and we genuinely care about making it right."

Compensation: Righting the Wrong

However, words alone do not suffice. To truly regain trust, actions speak louder than words. Compensation is a critical part of the equation. It's about righting the wrong, and it varies depending on the nature and severity of the error.

When considering compensation, it's important to remember that it's not just about the monetary value; it's about showing customers that you value their satisfaction. Compensation can take various forms:

- Monetary Compensation: This is the most straightforward form of compensation, where customers receive refunds, discounts, or credits for future purchases. It's a way of acknowledging the inconvenience and financial impact the issue may have caused.

- Gifts and Tokens: Sometimes, a small, unexpected gesture can go a long way. Sending a personalized gift, such as a handwritten note, a coupon for a free item, or a small token of appreciation, can make customers feel valued and cared for.

- Service Upgrades: In cases where the issue pertains to a service, offering an upgrade or extra service can be a meaningful way to compensate. For instance, a hotel might upgrade a guest to a higher room category or offer additional services at no cost.

- Problem Resolution: Beyond tangible compensation, swift and effective problem resolution is a form of compensation. It's about addressing the issue promptly, without causing additional stress or inconvenience to the customer.

While compensation is important, it's equally crucial to ensure that the same mistake doesn't happen again. This means conducting a thorough investigation, identifying the root cause, and implementing measures to prevent a recurrence.

Rebuilding Trust Through Transparency

Trust, once shattered, is a fragile thing. It can take a considerable effort to rebuild. Transparency is one of the most potent tools in this endeavor. Transparency means being open and honest about what went wrong and how you're addressing it.

Acknowledging the Mistake

The first step is acknowledging the mistake. It's surprising how many businesses, when faced with a crisis, try to downplay or even deny the problem. This approach erodes trust further. Transparency requires admitting the issue, no matter how embarrassing it may be.

Imagine a scenario in which a restaurant accidentally serves a dish with an ingredient to which a customer is allergic. Instead of denying the problem or trying to shift blame, a transparent response would involve immediately acknowledging the error, apologizing sincerely, and outlining the steps being taken to prevent such incidents in the future.

Communication and Updates

Transparency also involves keeping the affected customers, as well as the broader audience, informed about the progress in resolving the issue. Regular updates, communicated through various channels such as email, social media, or the company's website, demonstrate a commitment to addressing the problem.

For example, if an airline experiences a major delay due to unforeseen circumstances, being transparent about the cause, the expected duration of the delay, and the steps being taken to accommodate affected passengers can make a significant difference in how customers perceive the situation.

Learning from Mistakes

Transparency doesn't stop at acknowledging the mistake and providing updates. It extends to demonstrating a willingness to learn from the error. This means conducting an internal review to understand what led to the issue and taking steps to prevent its recurrence.

The transparency here comes from sharing the lessons learned and the concrete measures being implemented to prevent a similar crisis in the future. It shows customers that the company takes their concerns seriously and is committed to improvement.

Case Studies of Successful Customer Recovery

To illustrate the power of effective crisis management and customer recovery, let's delve into real-world case studies where companies faced significant challenges and managed to regain customer trust successfully.

Case Study 1: Johnson & Johnson's Tylenol Recall

In 1982, Johnson & Johnson faced a nightmare scenario when seven people died in the Chicago area after consuming cyanide-laced Tylenol capsules. The company immediately recalled 31 million bottles of Tylenol, costing them approximately $100 million.

What made this a remarkable case of customer recovery was the company's transparency, swift action, and commitment to public safety. Johnson & Johnson put customer safety above all else and openly communicated the risks. They introduced tamper-evident packaging to prevent similar incidents in the future. Their commitment to transparency and safety not only restored trust but set a standard for crisis management.

Case Study 2: Airbnb's Trust and Safety Measures

Airbnb, an online marketplace for lodging, faced a series of highly publicized incidents where guests encountered safety issues. In response, Airbnb implemented a comprehensive trust and safety program. They introduced measures such as host identity verification, guest screening, and a 24/7 support line.

By being transparent about the steps they were taking to enhance safety, Airbnb regained the trust of both hosts and guests. Their commitment to addressing these issues head-on and their ongoing transparency in sharing safety improvements showcased a dedication to customer security.

Case Study 3: Amazon's Handling of the 2013 Christmas Eve Outage

In 2013, Amazon experienced an outage on Christmas Eve, affecting its cloud services and leading to disruptions for numerous websites. What stood out in Amazon's response was their transparency about the cause of the outage, their communication throughout the recovery process, and their commitment to preventing future incidents.

Amazon offered detailed post-incident reports, and they implemented measures to enhance their infrastructure's resilience. This transparency not only helped them recover customer trust but also demonstrated their dedication to reliability and continuous improvement.

These case studies illustrate that, with the right approach, even the most challenging crises can be turned into opportunities for rebuilding customer trust. Transparency, swift action, and a commitment to improvement are central to successful customer recovery.

9.3 Proactive Issue Prevention

In the relentless world of business, the tides can turn in the blink of an eye. Customers, despite your best efforts, can occasionally encounter issues that leave them dissatisfied. It's in those moments of turbulence that your ability to recover and emerge stronger than before truly defines your brand. But, what if you could stop the storm before it even starts? What if you could navigate the treacherous waters of customer concerns with a proactive mindset?

This section delves into the realm of Proactive Issue Prevention, where we will explore the crucial art of anticipating, analyzing, and addressing potential problems. In the domain of customer-centricity, preparation is the key to resilience. By understanding the patterns and trends of past issues, implementing preventative measures, and fortifying your business for future challenges, you can become a true master of crisis management.

Analyzing Patterns and Trends

It begins with a simple yet profound question: What can the past teach us about the future? The answer, it turns out, is quite a lot. In the quest for proactive issue prevention, the first step is to analyze the patterns and trends that emerge from previous customer concerns.

Customer data is your treasure trove. Every complaint, every inquiry, every interaction holds valuable insights. Dive into this data with a critical eye. Identify recurring issues, the root causes, and the trigger points. Are there certain products or services that seem to generate more problems? Do specific departments or processes consistently lead to customer dissatisfaction?

The goal here is to create a comprehensive map of the customer journey, noting where potential pitfalls may lurk. This is not a mere statistical exercise; it's an exercise in empathy. You are putting yourself in your customers' shoes, experiencing their frustrations, and identifying the cracks in the pavement.

Once the patterns and trends are clear, the next step is to prioritize them. Not all issues are created equal, and focusing on the most significant pain points will yield the greatest returns. By analyzing past issues systematically, you're taking a proactive stance to prevent future complications.

Implementing Preventative Measures

Now that you've identified the patterns and trends, it's time to roll up your sleeves and get to work on implementing preventative measures. Proactivity isn't just about spotting the storm clouds; it's about fortifying your structure to withstand them.

Start by pinpointing the root causes of recurrent problems. It's not enough to treat the symptoms; you must address the underlying issues. Suppose you've discovered that a particular product consistently generates customer complaints due to a design flaw. In that case, it's not about just resolving individual complaints; it's about redesigning the product to eliminate the source of the problem.

Implementing preventative measures also requires a robust feedback loop. Actively seek out the insights and suggestions of your employees who are on the front lines, interacting with customers daily. Their perspectives are invaluable in understanding where improvements can be made.

Equally crucial is communication. Ensure that every member of your team, from customer service to product development, is aware of the preventative measures in place. This unified front not only reinforces the customer-centric culture but also empowers your employees to be part of the solution.

Building Resilience for Future Challenges

Proactive issue prevention doesn't stop at identifying patterns and implementing measures. It's about building resilience, preparing your organization to weather future storms and emerge stronger.

One key aspect of resilience is adaptability. Embrace change as a constant. As you evolve, so do your customers' needs and expectations. Stay vigilant by monitoring emerging trends and technological advancements. Being open to innovation and willing to adapt your processes will put you ahead of potential challenges.

Resilience is also about acknowledging that mistakes will happen. No matter how diligent your preventative measures, some issues may still surface. The difference is in how you respond. View each issue as an opportunity to learn and grow. Collect feedback, refine processes, and continuously improve.

Lastly, building resilience means fostering a culture of ownership. Encourage all team members to take responsibility for the customer experience. Each employee is a stakeholder in preventing issues and ensuring customer satisfaction. Empower them to make decisions that prioritize the customer's best interests.

In the world of business, challenges are inevitable, but crises are not. Through proactive issue prevention, your organization can be the captain of its destiny. You become the master of your own fate, charting a course to not only weather the storm but to sail forward, guided by the lessons of the past and the resilience of the future.

Chapter 10: Data-Driven Customer Relationship Management

10.1 The Role of Data in Understanding Customer Behavior

In today's dynamic business landscape, data reigns supreme. It serves as the compass guiding organizations through the ever-shifting tides of consumer preferences and behaviors. Within the realm of customer relationship management (CRM), understanding customer behavior is a critical component of success. In this section, we'll delve into the pivotal role that data plays in comprehending the intricate dance of customer behavior.

Customer Data: Types and Sources

Data is the lifeblood of modern business operations, and it comes in various forms. To gain insights into customer behavior, it's crucial to grasp the types and sources of customer data.

Customer data can be categorized into several key types:

- Demographic Data: These are the bare bones of customer information, encompassing age, gender, location, income, and other fundamental statistics. It provides a foundational understanding of your customer base.

- Behavioral Data: This category delves into customer actions and interactions. It includes data on past purchases, website visits, click-through rates, and social media engagement. Behavioral data unveils how customers engage with your brand.

- Psychographic Data: Here, we explore the less tangible aspects of your customers' personalities. Their interests, lifestyles, values, and motivations all fall under the umbrella of psychographic data. It helps you paint a more vivid picture of your customers.

- Transactional Data: This type hones in on financial interactions. It details each transaction—what was bought, when, and for how much. It's instrumental in understanding purchase patterns and product preferences.

Data sources are equally diverse. They can be categorized as:

- First-Party Data: The data you collect directly from your customers through interactions with your website, apps, or surveys.

- Second-Party Data: Information shared between trusted partners, which can augment your own first-party data.

- Third-Party Data: Data acquired from external sources, like data brokers, that can provide additional context and enrichment to your customer profiles.

Understanding the various types and sources of customer data empowers your organization to gather, curate, and utilize it effectively. When applied judiciously, it's akin to peering through a magnifying glass at the ever-evolving mosaic of customer behavior.

Customer Segmentation and Profiling

One of the most potent applications of customer data lies in segmentation and profiling. Think of it as the art of dividing your diverse customer base into manageable, more homogenous groups. This segmentation is critical in understanding your customers on a deeper level.

Customer segmentation can be approached in multiple ways, each unveiling different facets of customer behavior:

- Demographic Segmentation: Here, customers are grouped by age, gender, location, or income. It's akin to organizing puzzle pieces by their edges—a good start, but far from the whole picture.

- Behavioral Segmentation: In this method, customers are grouped by their actions. Are they frequent shoppers, occasional visitors, or cart abandoners? It's akin to classifying puzzle pieces based on their shapes, taking you closer to completing the puzzle.

- Psychographic Segmentation: By understanding the values, interests, and lifestyles of your customers, you're sorting puzzle pieces based on the images they form, revealing a much more vivid picture.

Once segmented, customer profiling adds depth. It's akin to putting the individual puzzle pieces together to see the entire landscape. Customer profiles include detailed information about individual customers within a segment, from their purchase history to their preferences and even their aspirations.

The magic happens when you combine segmentation and profiling. You're no longer observing random puzzle pieces; you're gazing at a clear, detailed image of each customer segment. This understanding enables you to tailor your strategies to their unique behaviors, wants, and needs, driving a more personalized and effective customer experience.

Predicting Customer Needs Through Data

In the ever-evolving realm of customer behavior, businesses need to be proactive, not reactive. Data, when harnessed correctly, has the power to anticipate customer needs and desires before customers even express them.

Predictive analytics is the crystal ball of the modern business world. It takes historical data, processes it through sophisticated algorithms, and generates insights into what customers are likely to do next. Here's how it works:

- Data Collection: The first step involves collecting a vast array of data, including customer interactions, purchase histories, website behaviors, and even external factors like market trends and competitor movements.

- Data Processing: Advanced algorithms and machine learning models take this data and dissect it. They identify patterns, trends, and correlations, sifting through the noise to find the signal.

- Predictive Insights: Armed with this processed data, businesses can predict what customers are likely to do next. This can range from predicting the products they might be interested in to the likelihood of them churning to competitors.

The beauty of predictive analytics is that it enables you to be proactive in meeting customer needs. It's like knowing the next move on the chessboard before your opponent makes it. With this knowledge, you can prepare tailor-made offers, content, or solutions, creating a seamless and delightful customer experience.

Data is the linchpin in your way to understand customer behavior. It comes in various forms, from the foundational demographic data to the intricate psychographic insights. Once harnessed, data allows you to segment and profile your customers, providing a clearer picture of their unique behaviors and preferences. Beyond that, predictive analytics opens the door to anticipating customer needs, enabling you to stay one step ahead. With data as your compass, you're equipped to navigate the intricate landscape of customer behavior, ensuring your strategies remain finely tuned to meet evolving customer expectations.

10.2 Measuring the Impact of Customer-Centric Strategies

In the ever-evolving landscape of business, one thing remains constant: the importance of data-driven decision-making. This chapter delves into the heart of the matter - measuring the impact of customer-centric strategies. After all, what good are these strategies if we can't quantify their success? It's time to roll up our sleeves, dive into the numbers, and decipher the metrics that truly matter.

Key Metrics for Customer Satisfaction

Customer satisfaction is the cornerstone of a thriving business. It's the litmus test for how well you're meeting your customers' needs. To measure it effectively, we need a set of key metrics that leave no room for ambiguity.

Net Promoter Score (NPS): Let's start with the big one. NPS measures customer loyalty by asking a simple question: "On a scale of 0 to 10, how likely are you to recommend our product/service to a friend or colleague?" The power of the NPS lies in its simplicity. Scores of 9 or 10 are your loyal promoters; 7 or 8 are passive; and 6 or below are detractors. The NPS metric paints a clear picture of how your customers view your brand.

Customer Satisfaction Score (CSAT): Sometimes, you need a direct answer. CSAT does just that. It asks customers to rate their satisfaction with your product or service, typically on a scale of 1 to 5. High scores indicate contentment, while low scores signal dissatisfaction. Keeping a close eye on your CSAT score helps you understand the immediate impact of your customer-centric strategies.

Customer Effort Score (CES): Customers appreciate a smooth and hassle-free experience. CES assesses how easy it is for customers to achieve their goals when interacting with your business. The less effort required, the happier the customer. By tracking CES, you can pinpoint areas where you need to simplify processes and enhance convenience.

Customer Lifetime Value (CLV)

Every business dreams of customers for life. Customer Lifetime Value (CLV) quantifies the total value a customer brings to your business during their entire relationship with you.

Calculating Customer Lifetime Value (CLV) is essential for understanding the long-term value of a customer to your business. It helps you determine how much you can invest in acquiring and retaining customers. Here's a simplified example of how to calculate CLV:

Step 1: Calculate Average Purchase Value

First, calculate the average purchase value, which is the average amount a customer spends on each purchase. Let's assume that, on average, a customer spends $50 per transaction.

Step 2: Calculate Average Purchase Frequency

Next, calculate how often, on average, a customer makes a purchase within a specific time frame. Suppose the average customer makes a purchase four times a year.

Step 3: Calculate Customer Value Per Year

To find the customer value per year, multiply the average purchase value by the average purchase frequency. In our example, it's $50 (average purchase value) * 4 (average purchase frequency) = $200 per year.

Step 4: Determine Average Customer Lifespan

The average customer lifespan is the average number of years a customer remains active and makes purchases. For this example, let's assume the average customer remains a customer for five years.

Step 5: Calculate CLV

Now, to calculate the CLV, you simply multiply the customer value per year by the average customer lifespan. In this case, it's $200 (customer value per year) * 5 (average customer lifespan) = $1,000.

So, the CLV for this example is $1,000. This means that, on average, a customer is worth $1,000 to your business over the course of their five-year relationship with your company.

It's important to note that this is a simplified example, and in reality, CLV calculations can become more complex by considering factors like customer acquisition costs, retention rates, and different customer segments. However, this basic formula provides a starting point for understanding the value of your customers over time and can be adapted to suit the specifics of your business.

Understanding CLV is like having a crystal ball that reveals the future revenue potential of your customer base. Here's how to make sense of it:

Historical CLV: Start by calculating the historical CLV, which tells you how much a customer has spent during their time as your customer. This data can guide marketing strategies and highlight the value of long-term relationships.

Predictive CLV: Predictive analytics can take CLV to the next level. By analyzing past customer behavior, you can forecast the potential revenue from individual customers over time. This predictive insight enables you to tailor your approach to high-value customers and maximize their CLV.

Customer Segmentation: CLV isn't one-size-fits-all. Segment your customers based on their CLV to create personalized strategies. High-CLV customers may receive exclusive offers, while low-CLV customers might benefit from retention efforts.

ROI of Customer-Centric Investments

In business, you invest to reap returns. Customer-centric strategies are no exception. To assess their effectiveness, you must calculate the Return on Investment (ROI). It's the nitty-gritty of determining whether your investments are paying off and how to make smart financial decisions.

Customer Acquisition Cost (CAC): The foundation of ROI is understanding how much it costs to acquire a new customer. The CAC encompasses all expenses related to marketing, sales, and onboarding for a new customer. Keep this number in check, and your ROI will be poised for success.

Customer Retention Cost (CRC): On the flip side, retaining existing customers often comes at a lower cost. Calculate the CRC by factoring in the expenses related to customer support, loyalty programs, and other retention strategies. A lower CRC indicates that your customer-centric initiatives are paying off.

Customer Lifetime Value (CLV): Remember CLV? It's your trump card for ROI. Compare the CLV with CAC and CRC. If the CLV significantly exceeds these costs, you're in a winning position. For every dollar invested in acquiring and retaining customers, you're generating a healthy return.

Customer Feedback Integration: ROI isn't just about dollars; it's also about creating value for your customers. Integrate their feedback into your strategies. Ask for their input and insights. When customers feel heard and see changes based on their feedback, their loyalty and lifetime value increase.

Employee Training and Customer-Centric Culture: Invest in your employees. Well-trained, motivated staff members play a pivotal role in executing customer-centric strategies. Measure the ROI of employee training by tracking metrics like employee satisfaction, customer satisfaction, and efficiency improvements.

The world of data-driven customer relationship management is one of precision and predictability. It's the realm where smart businesses leverage data to make informed decisions, enhance customer satisfaction, and maximize their ROI. In these metrics lie the secrets to understanding the success of your customer-centric strategies. By mastering them, you unlock the true potential of your business and convert customer data into actionable insights.

10.3 Ethical Data Usage and Privacy

In the age of data, where information flows ceaselessly, the responsibility of handling customer data is paramount. Businesses now possess an unprecedented ability to understand their customers on a granular level, which, when used responsibly, can result in personalized, meaningful interactions. However, in this realm of data-driven customer relationship management, ethics and privacy stand as cornerstones, essential to maintaining trust and integrity.

Respecting Customer Privacy

Respecting customer privacy is not just a legal obligation; it is a moral imperative. It's about acknowledging that every piece of data you collect represents a real individual—a person with fears, dreams, and a life beyond their interactions with your brand. To respect customer privacy means to safeguard their personal information, never overstepping boundaries, and providing complete transparency.

Think of it as a pact of trust. Customers entrust you with their data with the understanding that you will use it responsibly. Respecting their privacy involves a few fundamental principles:

Transparency: Transparency is the foundation of trust. Be upfront about what data you collect, why you collect it, and how it will be used. Your customers should know precisely what they're signing up for.

Consent: Seek permission. Before collecting any data, ask for explicit consent. Make it easy for your customers to opt in or out. It's their data, after all.

Data Minimization: Collect only what is necessary. The more data you have, the more responsibility you bear. Limit your data collection to the essentials required to serve your customers better.

Security: Protect the data as if it were gold. Implement robust security measures to guard against breaches. Data breaches erode trust, and trust, once lost, is challenging to regain.

Data Security and Compliance

Data security is not a one-time effort; it's an ongoing commitment. Your customers trust you to keep their information safe. Breaching that trust can result in severe consequences. This section dives deeper into the vital aspect of data security and compliance.

Encryption: Data should be stored securely and transmitted in an encrypted format. Encryption ensures that even if unauthorized access occurs, the data remains unreadable and unusable.

Access Control: Limit access to customer data. Only those who need it for legitimate purposes should be able to access it. Implement strict access controls to prevent unauthorized use.

Regular Audits: Conduct routine audits to assess the security of your data storage and processing systems. Identify vulnerabilities and address them promptly.

Compliance: Compliance with data protection laws is not optional. Familiarize yourself with regulations like GDPR or CCPA, and ensure your practices adhere to their requirements.

Incident Response Plan: Be prepared for the worst. Have a well-defined incident response plan in place to mitigate the impact of data breaches should they occur.

Maintaining Trust in Data-Driven CRM

Maintaining trust in data-driven customer relationship management is a continuous effort. Trust, once gained, can be fragile, and it's challenging to rebuild once broken. The steps you take to respect customer privacy and ensure data security lay the foundation for trust, but maintaining it is an ongoing commitment.

Accountability: As a business, you are accountable for the data you collect and how you use it. Own up to any mistakes or breaches promptly, and take responsibility for remediation.

Regular Communication: Keep the lines of communication open with your customers. Update them on how their data is used and any changes to your data practices. Transparency is key.

Customer Control: Give your customers control over their data. Allow them to access, correct, or delete their information. This not only complies with regulations but also fosters trust.

Education: Educate your employees about the importance of data privacy and security. They play a critical role in upholding customer trust.

Ethical Decision-Making: Embed ethical decision-making into your organizational culture. Ensure that every team member understands the importance of ethics and privacy in data-driven CRM.

In a world where data drives decisions, building and maintaining trust is a competitive advantage. Customers who trust you with their data are more likely to engage, recommend your brand, and remain loyal. However, this trust is delicate and must be nurtured through ethical data usage and a commitment to customer privacy. Data-driven CRM can revolutionize how you connect with your customers, but it's the ethical foundation that will keep those connections strong and lasting. Your customers aren't just data points; they are individuals who deserve respect and protection. In this digital age, that respect and protection are the ultimate currencies of trust, and they are what will set your brand apart as a beacon of integrity in the realm of data-driven customer relationship management.

Chapter 11: Interactive Elements for Self-Assessment

11.1 Self-Assessment Quizzes

In your way to become a customer magnet, it's imperative to understand where you stand on the spectrum of customer-centricity. Are you truly putting your customers at the core of your business strategy, or is there room for improvement? To help you gain clarity on your customer-centricity journey, we've crafted a series of self-assessment quizzes.

Customer-Centricity Quiz

This quiz delves into the very essence of your approach to customer relationships. Answer these questions honestly, as your responses will shed light on whether your business truly revolves around your customers or if there's room for enhancement.

1. Customer-Centric Mission: On a scale of 1 to 5, how well can you articulate your organization's mission, which is centered around meeting customer needs and expectations?

2. Customer Feedback Integration: How often do you actively seek and incorporate customer feedback into your business operations, products, and services?

3. Customer Empathy: Rate your organization's ability to understand and empathize with the challenges, desires, and aspirations of your customers.

4. Employee Alignment: On a scale of 1 to 5, how well do your employees align with your customer-centric mission? Are they actively engaged in fulfilling customer needs?

5. Flexibility and Adaptability: To what extent does your organization adapt and evolve based on changing customer preferences and market dynamics?

6. Customer-Centric Culture: Do you have clear strategies and initiatives in place to foster a customer-centric culture throughout your organization?

7. Customer Retention: How satisfied are you with your customer retention rates? Are customers returning for repeat business?

8. Customer Advocacy: Do you actively encourage and support customers to become brand advocates who promote your products or services?

As you complete this quiz, remember that there are no right or wrong answers. The aim is to provide you with a snapshot of your organization's current customer-centricity level. You'll then be equipped to identify areas where you excel and those that may require further attention.

Customer Experience Evaluation
Understanding how your customers perceive their interactions with your business is crucial. This self-assessment will help you gauge your current customer experience and identify areas for improvement.

1. Customer Satisfaction: On a scale of 1 to 5, how satisfied do you believe your customers are with their overall experience when interacting with your business?

2. Ease of Doing Business: How easy is it for customers to make a purchase or engage with your business? Rate it on a scale of 1 to 5.

3. Response Time: How quickly does your organization respond to customer inquiries and issues? Are response times meeting customer expectations?

4. Consistency: Are you confident that the customer experience is consistent across different touchpoints and interactions with your business?

5. Personalization: To what extent do you tailor your interactions to individual customer preferences, needs, and histories?

6. Customer Loyalty: How likely is it that your customers will return for future business or recommend your services to others?

7. Resolution of Issues: How effectively do you handle and resolve customer issues and complaints?

8. Feedback Collection: Do you actively collect feedback from customers to gain insights into their experiences?

The results of this assessment will offer a clearer understanding of how customers perceive your business, and it can guide you in enhancing their experiences.

Measuring Your Customer Advocacy

Customer advocacy can be a powerful force in your business's growth. Understanding where you currently stand in terms of customer advocacy is pivotal in converting loyal customers into your sales force.

1. Advocate Identification: How many of your existing customers actively recommend your products or services to others?

2. Advocate Engagement: On a scale of 1 to 5, how engaged are your advocates in promoting your business?

3. Referral Program Effectiveness: If you have a referral program, how successful has it been in driving new customers through existing customer referrals?

4. Customer Testimonials: How many customers have provided testimonials or reviews that reflect positively on your products or services?

5. Advocate Content Sharing: To what extent do your advocates share your content, such as blog posts, social media updates, or promotional materials?

6. Advocate Feedback: How frequently do you seek feedback from your advocates on how to enhance their advocacy efforts?

By answering these questions, you'll gain insight into your current level of customer advocacy and can subsequently work on strategies to amplify it.

These self-assessment quizzes are designed to provide you with a realistic snapshot of your customer-centricity, customer experience, and advocacy efforts. Armed with this information, you can make informed decisions on how to further attract and retain loyal customers and, most importantly, convert them into your most enthusiastic sales force. Remember, the path to customer magnetism starts with understanding your current position and taking steps to improve.

11.2 Checklists for Implementation

Businesses often find themselves at a crossroads to pursuit of customer-centric excellence. They've read the manuals, attended seminars, and perhaps even implemented a few customer-centric initiatives. But how can they be certain they're on the right path? That's where checklists come into play. A well-constructed checklist is more than just a list of to-dos; it's a guide to success, a roadmap to ensure that your customer-centric efforts are not only on the right track but are also setting you apart from the competition.

Customer-Centric Action Checklist

Picture this: your business is a finely tuned machine, every cog and gear working in harmony to deliver exceptional customer experiences. How do you ensure that all these components are aligned? With a Customer-Centric Action Checklist.

Key Point 1: Defining the Customer-Centric Vision

Start by clearly defining your customer-centric vision. It's not about vague statements or aspirations; it's about articulating precisely what customer-centricity means for your business. Your vision should be a beacon, guiding every decision and action.

Key Point 2: Empowering Your Workforce

One of the most significant assets in your quest for customer-centricity is your workforce. This point is about creating a culture where employees are not just working but also passionately embracing the concept of customer-centricity. It involves training, empowering, and encouraging them to make decisions in the best interest of your customers.

Key Point 3: Continuous Feedback Loops

Customer feedback is your compass. Ensure you have robust systems in place for collecting and analyzing feedback from every interaction. Feedback is not just about complaint resolution; it's about learning and adapting to ever-changing customer needs and expectations.

Crisis Management Preparedness
Picture this: you've been navigating the waters of customer-centricity smoothly, but then a storm hits. A crisis emerges,

and your response could make or break customer trust. Crisis management preparedness is your life jacket in such situations.

Key Point 1: Identifying Potential Crisis Points

The first step is to identify potential crisis points within your customer journey. Anticipate where things could go wrong and have a plan in place. It's about being proactive rather than reactive. Your customers will appreciate that you've considered their well-being.

Key Point 2: Effective Communication Strategies

In times of crisis, communication is your lifeline. Customers need to know that you're on top of the situation and working towards resolution. Have a clear communication plan that addresses not only the problem but also what you're doing to rectify it.

Key Point 3: Learning and Improvement

Once the storm has passed, it's time to evaluate. What went well? What could have been handled better? This step is about extracting lessons from the crisis and using them to improve your processes and prevent similar issues in the future.

Data-Driven CRM Readiness

Picture this: your business is a treasure trove of customer data. But, what good is data if you don't know how to use it effectively? Data-driven CRM readiness ensures that your data is not just collected, but leveraged to deliver superior customer experiences.

Key Point 1: Comprehensive Data Collection

Before you can become data-driven, you must ensure that you're collecting comprehensive and accurate data. This means more than just customer names and contact information. It's about understanding their behaviors, preferences, and pain points.

Key Point 2: Analyzing and Actionable Insights

Data, on its own, is just a pile of numbers and statistics. This key point emphasizes the importance of turning raw data into actionable insights. You should be able to look at your data and say, "Aha, this is what our customers need, and this is how we can deliver it better."

Key Point 3: Data Privacy and Security

Customer data is a sensitive matter, and in today's world, data privacy is of paramount importance. Ensure that your data practices are not only compliant with regulations but also that you go above and beyond to protect your customers' information. A data breach can undo all your customer-centric efforts in an instant.

These checklists are not just tools for self-assessment; they are your compass in the ever-changing landscape of customer-centricity. They provide a tangible roadmap to steer your business toward success. The path to customer-centric excellence may not always be straightforward, but with these checklists as your guide, you'll be well-prepared for the journey ahead. Your customers will thank you for it with their loyalty and advocacy.

Conclusion

As we conclude this exploration of customer-centricity, it's not just the end of a book but the start of a transformative phase in your business and professional life. What you've learned here is not mere knowledge; it's a set of tools and strategies to reshape your customer relationships.

Throughout these pages, we've delved into the fundamental principles of customer-centricity. You've come to appreciate the importance of focusing on customers, showing empathy, and creating exceptional experiences.

You've unveiled strategies for collecting customer feedback, implementing loyalty programs, and personalizing your communication. You've grasped the significance of customer advocacy, social proof, and exceeding customer expectations.

But our work doesn't end here. Customer magnetism is not a static concept. It evolves as your business grows and as customer preferences change. It demands a commitment to constant learning and adaptation. Here are some key takeaways to guide you on your path to customer magnetism:

1. Listening Matters: Customer feedback is invaluable. Pay attention to your customers, their needs, and their concerns. Improvement begins with understanding your customers.

2. Be Flexible: The business landscape changes, and so do your customers. Be adaptable to new technologies, trends,

and customer preferences. Be responsive to remain a magnetic force in the market.

3. Prioritize Ethics: Trust is at the core of customer magnetism. Uphold ethical practices, maintain transparency, and make decisions that prioritize your customers' well-being.

4. Data-Driven Decision-Making: Rely on data to guide your decisions. Measure the impact of your strategies and use data to refine your approach.

5. Encourage Advocacy: Your loyal customers can become your best salesforce. Encourage them to advocate for your brand through referral programs and exceptional service.

6. Stay Informed: Stay aware of emerging trends, technologies, and shifts in the marketplace. Be the first to adapt and meet the evolving demands of your customers.

7. Invest in Your Team: Train and empower your employees to embody your customer-centric values. Their commitment to customer satisfaction is crucial.

8. Keep Your Commitments: Exceed customer expectations. Consistency in quality and value is vital.

9. Embrace Technology: Technology can enhance the customer experience, but never let it overshadow the human touch that customers value.

10. Customer Focus: Make customer-centricity a core value of your organization. Every decision and action should aim to create a positive impact on your customers.

As we part ways, remember that these principles are about action, not just theory. Turn knowledge into execution, and create a customer-centric culture that sets you apart in your industry.

These principles will be uniquely yours. Implement them, measure your progress, and adapt them to your context. With these tools, you're not just in business; you're in the business of creating loyal customers who will become your most ardent supporters and advocates.

Your dedication to understanding and implementing these principles is a testament to your commitment to excellence. As you step out into the world of business and customer engagement, remember that you have the power to attract and retain loyal customers, to build lasting relationships, and to shape the future of your business.

www.ingramcontent.com/pod-product-compliance
Lightning Source LLC
Chambersburg PA
CBHW070115010626
45794CB00013B/1631